Paranormal
DUNDEE

Fish Street looking East

Paranormal
DUNDEE

GEOFF HOLDER

The
History
Press

To the DJCA Electronic Imaging crowd, Class of '91

Frontispiece:
Murraygate in the nineteenth century. *(Perth & Kinross Libraries)*

First published 2010

The History Press
The Mill, Brimscombe Port
Stroud, Gloucestershire, GL5 2QG
www.thehistorypress.co.uk

British Library Cataloguing in Publication Data.
A catalogue record for this book is available from the British Library.

ISBN 978 0 7524 5419 1

Typesetting and origination by The History Press
Printed in Great Britain
Manufacturing managed by Jellyfish Print Solutions Ltd

CONTENTS

ACKNOWLEDGEMENTS

There is a special heaven reserved for librarians, and I strongly suspect the local studies staff of the A.K. Bell Library in Perth and the Dundee Central Library will end up there for services to this book. I am also grateful to the respective library services for permission to reproduce a number of images. My thanks also go out to Ailsa Lawson and Nick Cook, the kind of enthusiasts who make the world a better place, and to Steve Hammond for the insight into the work of ASUFORA. Ségolène Dupuy toiled above and beyond the call of duty in the digital darkroom. Respect is also due to all the authors quoted or referred to: their good works are listed in the Bibliography, and are well worth exploring.

This book is part of a series of works by Geoff Holder dedicated to the mysterious and paranormal. For more information, or to contribute your own experience, please visit www.geoffholder.co.uk

INTRODUCTION

If you take an old map of the centre of Dundee and rotate it through 90 degrees the street plan resembles a dancing human figure, the four principal streets forming the arms and legs and the steeple of St Mary's Church positioned at the head. This 'map simulacrum' was first noticed in 1678 by Robert Edward, the minister of Murroes, who went on to match body parts with the geography: the stomach was the market-place, with the market cross at the navel; the intestines were at the 'shambles', where animals were butchered and blood and guts flowed in the street; and, stated rather demurely, a culverted burn represented the urino-genitary system.

In some ways performing a similar change of perspective allows us to understand modern Dundee. To many, the name of the city conjures up images of a forest of tall smoking chimneys and a choking ring of Victorian jute and linen mills, a grimy industrial working-class city *par excellence*. For others, what comes to mind is the urban wasteland of the post-industrial crash, with all its attendant problems. Yet this was not always how Dundee was perceived. It was once one of the great cities of medieval Scotland, importing wine and grain from southern Europe and exporting hides and woollen goods to the Baltic states. Despite suffering war, famine and plague, by the eighteenth century it had a thriving harbour, a busy maritime quarter and a number of gracious, elegant houses within its walled confines. Sadly, a series of poor planning decisions saw the harbour decline, the infrastructure weaken, and the medieval core disintegrate. What was once a historic cityscape to rival Edinburgh's Old Town was swept away, leaving an architectural legacy that – with a few significant exceptions – was of poor quality, and which is only now

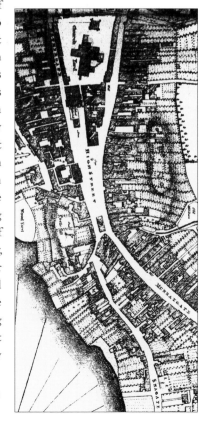

The 'dancing man' that can be made out in the medieval street plan. *(Perth & Kinross Libraries)*

7

Dundee's busy harbour in the seventeenth century. *(Perth & Kinross Libraries)*

being slowly regenerated, with notable expansions in the areas of university education and medical biotechnology.

Somewhere under the shopping malls and ring roads, however, there lurks an alternative city, a place of legends and lore, of stories of the strange and the supernatural, the fantastic and the fabulous. For in terms of the paranormal and the peculiar, Dundee punches above its weight. Its history of magical practitioners and witch persecution is detailed in chapter one, which also sets out the 'truth' – as far as it can be known – of the infamous Grissel Jaffray. Chapter two discusses the modern phenomenon of UFOs, and shows that strange things have been seen in the sky over Dundee for a great many years. One of Dundee's great advantages is its link with the coastline and rural hinterland of Angus and eastern Perthshire, and this comes to the fore in chapter three, which details the incredible number of sightings of panthers, pumas and other exotic felines in the area. There are more animal shenanigans in the following chapter, which features long-distance dogs, indestructible cats, mystery toads, freaks of nature, a devil crab and hypnotised hyenas – not to mention something truly extraordinary allegedly found in the belly of the famous Tay Whale.

Dundee in 1678, seen from the north: Broughty Ferry Castle is on the left, Dudhope Castle to the right. In the centre is St Mary's steeple. The obscuring Corbie Hill was quarried away. *(Perth & Kinross Libraries)*

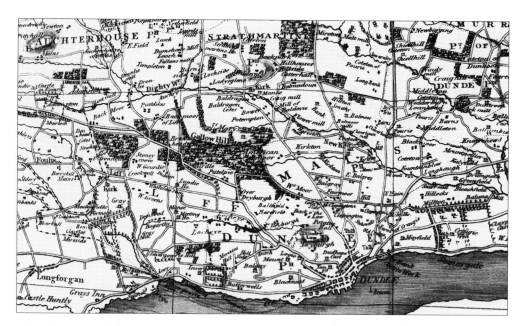

Above: Dundee and the surrounding parishes in 1822. Note how small the actual city is. *(Perth & Kinross Libraries)*

Right: A typical image of old Dundee before the wholesale urban redevelopment. *(Perth & Kinross Libraries)*

Chapter five, 'Rituals, Religion and Superstitions', covers such diverse topics as stone circles, fairy kidnapping, the Devil's boulders and the supernatural beliefs of whalers and working folk. Chapter six, 'Gothic Horrors', hosts a coffin-full of bodysnatchers, cannibals, murderers and supposed occult events, and manages to squeeze in vampires, zombies and *Frankenstein* for good measure. (Note that there are few ghosts mentioned here, because the subject will be covered in much greater detail in a later volume, *Haunted Dundee*.) And we finish off with 'Mysteries, Oddities and Weird Weather', which collects together some truly bizarre one-off stories.

So, take the dancing man by the hand, set the controls for the heart of the weird, and come and explore Paranormal Dundee.

Murraygate in the early twentieth century, after the aggrandisement of the centre. *(Perth & Kinross Libraries)*

The Tay Rail Bridge, taken from Dudhope Castle in 1909. Note the forest of industrial chimneystacks, most of which have now disappeared. *(Perth & Kinross Libraries)*

one

WITCHCRAFT

Grissel Jaffray

Come out, come out, foul witch Jaffray,
Or e'er the night return,
Thy body wirried at the stake,
In flames o' hell shall burn.

Come out, come out, Grizzel Jaffray,
Come out, come out, they cry;
Thy soul is barter'd to the de'il,
Thou hast the evil eye.

This rhyme appeared in *The City Echo*, a short-lived Dundee magazine published in 1909. By then Grissel Jaffray had achieved iconic, almost mythical status: she was Dundee's very own witch. Over the years she has been brandished as a symbol of feminism, as a victim of a brutal Presbyterian intolerance, and as an emblem of the indomitable spirit of Dundonian women. Despite her story being occasionally clouded by legend and make-believe, she was a real person, and in 1669 she was found guilty of the capital crime of witchcraft, tied to a stake, wirried (strangled to death), and her body burned to ashes.

It is not known what magical crimes were alleged against Grissel Jaffray, as the records are incomplete – so fragmentary, in fact, that at least one Victorian historian suggested the Council and/or the Presbytery had deliberately destroyed the incriminating documents. This, of course, can't be proved, but a few scraps of information have been preserved in various archives for us to build up at least a partial picture of the woman.

It appears she was married to James Butchart or Boutchard, described as a maltman (or brewer) in Dundee. James was a burgess of the city, having achieved this status at the age of twenty-one, and came from a long-established family of bakers. In modern terms, all this meant he would today be probably regarded as a lower middle-class tradesman, a member of his trade's guild, and in later life respected for several decades of experience. Not wealthy, but certainly not poor. (Some nineteenth-century writers claimed Grissel was married to a poor man named Ramsay and was a widow when she died; it is unclear where this alternative view comes from, as it is not backed up by the original records.) The couple lived, at least for a time, in Calendar Close, a little to the west of Long Wynd in the old Overgate (all now demolished). James was born in 1594; if Grissel was roughly the same age, she would have been seventy-five at her execution in 1669. Grissel and James survived the sack of Dundee by Montrose in 1645 and the even worse destruction inflicted by General Monck in 1651. They had lived through plague, pestilence, fire and famine. They deserved a peaceful old age; but that was not to be.

Other than a brief reference in a deed of 1663 to a Grissel Jaffray, the 'witch' herself does not appear in any documents until 11 November 1669, when the Privy Council, the highest judicial body in the land, recorded that she was incarcerated in the Tolbooth, under suspicion of the 'horrid crime of witchcraft.' The Council sent a carefully-worded letter from Edinburgh authorising the Dundee authorities to set up a Commission to try Grissel, and noted:

> If by her own confession, without any sort of torture or other indirect means used, it shall be found she hath renounced her baptism, entered into paction with the devil, or otherwise that malefices be legally proven against her, that then and no otherwise they cause the sentence of death to be executed upon her.

Malefices were evil deeds such as murder, assault, poisoning, theft or destruction of property or livestock, but distinguished from ordinary offences by being due to witchcraft. Malefices were often 'proved' by witnesses coming forward claiming that the 'witch' had cursed them or their animals. The renunciation of Christian baptism and making a pact with the Devil were knottier issues to prove legally, and typically depended on the accused making a confession (often under torture) or being implicated by another witch (who may also have been tortured, or even hoped the information would gain their release).

That was 11 November. On the 23rd a minute in the Council records noted in passing that 'Grissel Jaffray, witch' had been executed. So at some point between the 11th and the 23rd Grissel had been tried at the old Tolbooth, found guilty, and executed near the old market cross.

We can only guess what crimes she was charged with; the identity of the witnesses brought in to accuse her; whether or not she confessed; and what had led up to this terrible conclusion. Had Grissel been practicing folk magic and healing people and animals for decades? Did she know more about herbs, the weather and the ways of the natural world than many people thought 'canny'? We know the Presbytery of Dundee were engaged in a witchhunt because on 27 April 1669 they ordered all the Kirk Sessions in Dundee and the surrounding areas to take action against all those guilty of witchcraft – suspects were to be banished or handed over to the Magistrates. Had Grissel angered or offended a minister or some other prominent member of Dundee society? Or did her age-wizened face just 'fit'? We will never know.

The only thing the records show is that the Commission that tried her was made up of the cream of the Dundonian élite: John Tarbet, the Provost; John Kinloch, the Dean of Guild; Sir Alexander Wedderburn of Blackness; John Wedderburn of Blackness (a relative of Sir Alexander); Graham of Monorgan; Fothringham of Powrie; Mr Patrick Zeaman of Dryburgh; Henry Scrymsour, Minister of St Mary's; John Guthrie of the South Church; and Revd William Rait of the Third Charge (later St Paul's Church). Together this group of politicians, wealthy merchants, landed gentry and men of God condemned a seventy-five-year-old woman to death.

The plaque on Peter Street commemorating Grissel Jaffray, burned for witchcraft. *(Geoff Holder)*

The minute that off-handedly recorded Grissel's execution noted that she had accused several others of witchcraft, and the Provost, the Baillies, the Dean of Guild and the ministers were to take a meeting to decide what to do with these new suspects. What they did, on 8 February 1670, was to approve the ministers' request to employ a 'prover', a man who claimed he could identify witches, often by brutal means such as pricking; some of these witch-finders had successful careers, although often their charlatanry was eventually exposed. Despite the rubber-stamping of the use of the prover (and the cost for hiring him), there is no further indication that he was ever employed; and the 'witches' named by Grissel also disappear from the records. We do not even know their names, never mind what happened to them – although one of them was probably Margaret Coul (of whom more later). Perhaps someone in authority realised that a suspect under duress will say anything, and therefore that any information so gained was of dubious value. The Privy Council had, it is true, forbidden torture in Grissel's case; but perhaps she had been subjected to the 'non-physical' equivalent: sleep deprivation. It leaves no marks and causes no pain, but after several days being forcibly kept awake, you will say anything – *anything* – just to be granted some sleep. But as with everything else connected with Grissel, we can only speculate.

There is one more documented event, however. On 30 November 1669, perhaps some ten days or so after his wife was strangled and burned, the once prosperous maltman James Butchart petitioned to be admitted to the Hospital (Dundee's proto-workhouse or poorhouse). Seven days later the Council approved his application. Perhaps we can imagine a heartbroken, emotionally-shattered old man resigning himself to ending his life in poverty and shame.

Traditionally, the execution was thought to have taken place on a spot on Seagate. There is a modern plaque on the wall in the passage of Peter Street, and a cross marked in the cobbles at the lane's junction with Seagate, where the Market Cross was said to have stood. When the Jaffe Brothers' building was constructed further east in the 1850s, the laying of the foundations uncovered a large mound of wood ashes. Immediately the rumour went round that it was the very site where Grissel had been burned. The story – which was still being repeated fifty years later – shows the grip 'the Dundee Witch' has had on the city's collective imagination. However, all this has now been revealed to be mere fantasy: in their wonderful book *Lost Dundee* Charles McKean and Patricia Whatley have shown that the long-held notion that the original tolbooth and market cross stood at the foot of Peter Street is in fact a myth, derived from a badly translated Latin charter. From the earliest days of the burgh the market cross was located in the market place or High Street, and it was there that Grissel Jaffray met her fiery end.

There are several further instances of the way Grissel has become part of folklore and legend. Supposedly her only son became a ship's captain and returned to Dundee on the very day his mother was judicially murdered. According to the variant then told, he either publicly cursed the town and immediately set sail again, or fled in shame, changing his name because he did

Above: The alleged (but probably false) site of the Market Cross, off Seagate. *(Geoff Holder)*

Below: This detail from an 1858 map shows where the Market Cross, the site of Grissel Jaffray's execution, was thought to be. *(Perth & Kinross Libraries)*

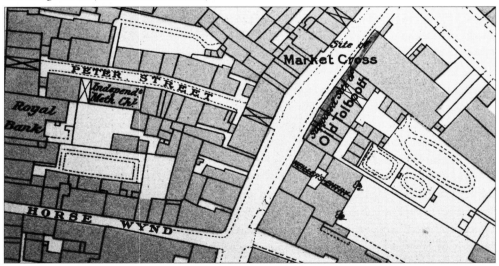

not want to be associated with a servant of Satan. The next part of the tale has him making a fortune in India, retiring to Scotland, buying the estate of Murie in the Carse of Gowrie, and founding the Yeaman dynasty of Murie. Successive historians have rubbished this as fantasy: there is no record of Grissel and James having a surviving son, and the Yeamans were a power in the land long before Grissel was executed.

A nineteenth-century view of the Market Cross on High Street. *(Perth & Kinross Libraries)*

Another strange story, as set out in Alex Warden's massive five-volume *Angus or Forfarshire, the Land and People, Descriptive and Historical*, is that Grissel supposedly planted a tree that grew to be the large ash just west of Ballumbie House, the mansion on the north-east edge of the city. The nineteenth-century house is on the site of Ballumbie Castle, but there is no obvious link with Grissel. The pub at 22 St Andrews Street was called *Grissel Jaffray's* for about ten years from 1994; William Blain's popular potboiler novel *Witch's Blood* features a witch named Elspet Renkyne whose life and execution is clearly based in part on Grissel; and in 1935 Philip Blair wrote a play called *Grissel Jaffray,* which was broadcast on the BBC (and which would make a splendid revival for a local drama company – there is a copy in the Local History Department of the Wellgate Library).

The most effective intrusion of Grissel Jaffray into the Dundee imagination, however, is Claire-Marie Watson's 2003 novel, *The Curewife*. Here the few known facts of Grissel's life are used as a structure to underpin a compelling tale of seventeenth-century Scotland, with one woman's struggle to earn a living set against a background of political and military turmoil, violence, plague and witchhunts. As shown in the title, Watson makes Grissel a 'curewife', a healer, midwife and practitioner of folk magic.

More Dundee witches

Grissel Jaffray has iconic status in Dundee partly because she is the only witch we know anything about, however little that may be. Unlike Perth, Forfar and Aberdeen, Dundee appears to have put very few witches to death – but that doesn't mean that it didn't happen, simply that we have such sparse records. For example, the City Treasurer's accounts for 1590/91 include the cost of burning a witch, although there is no other record of this execution, and we do not know the person's name or even if they were male or female. The total – covering the rope, creelfulls of coal, two tar barrels and the carriage – came to £5 16s 2d Scots (perhaps £1,000 in modern money), of which £1 Scots went to the hangman for his trouble. And a century before Grissel, in December 1569 – just six years after witchcraft became a capital crime under the new post-Reformation Protestant regime – the Regent, the 1st Earl of Moray, burned two people in St Andrews and then moved on to Dundee, where he had a 'company of witches' burned. We are given no names, no details of the convictions – we are not even told how many were in the 'company'.

Moray, incidentally, was not hunting down the witches himself; his was a quasi-royal progress around the country, and wherever he paused the authorities seemed to drag out some local miscreants, subject them to trial, and have the Regent add his authority to the executions. Also of interest is that Moray – who was ruling in the place of the deposed Mary Queen of Scots while her son James VI was still a child – was killed in January 1670 in what was the first recorded assassination by a gun.

The Kirk Session was the Church's frontline in the fight against alternative worldviews. Each parish had a Session consisting of the minister and the elders, and most Sundays after divine service these men would meet and dole out local justice, typically dealing with cases of fornication, non-attendance at church, swearing, neighbourhood disputes, domestic violence – and the practice of magic. Some Sessions were composed of fair-minded men trying to impose order in difficult situations; others were run by intolerant bigots. Most cases of magic – or 'charming' as it was usually termed – were dealt with by the Sessions themselves, and the punishments were relatively minor; if a case involved a high level of witchcraft, it was pushed up to the next levels of Church organisation, the Presbytery or the Synod. If the ministers were convinced the 'witch' was guilty of *malefices* or Satanic collusion, the suspect was handed over to the civic authorities, as only they had the legal right to execute people for breaking the law.

At her execution, Grissel Jaffray accused other people of being witches, but their names were not recorded. One likely candidate (because the dates fit) was Margaret Coul. Grissel died in November 1669; in the following February the ministers gained permission to pay for a witch-pricker; and the following month Margaret was being investigated first by the Dundee Presbytery and then, moving up the Church hierarchy, by the Synod of Angus and Mearns. The good folk of the Church then passed her on to the Dundee magistrates, who in turn wrote to the Lord Advocate asking for a Commission to try (and if necessary, execute) Margaret on charges of witchcraft. Whatever was the exact nature of the evidence presented to the Lord Advocate, he clearly did not think it made much of a case, and refused to grant a Commission. The Dundee magistrates therefore had no option but to drop all the charges, and Margaret was released in August 1670. The Church, foiled in its attempt to bring the 'witch' to what they saw as justice, promptly banished Margaret and some other unnamed suspects from the Presbytery's bounds (which meant the whole of Dundee and outlying villages). Although Margaret's case is frustrating because we know so little about it, at least it shows that in Scotland, witch trials, however unfair to our eyes, were actually conducted with full legal process: if a judge did not consider the evidence to be up to snuff, the trial did not go ahead.

In 1873 William Motherwell published a collection of Scottish ballads entitled *Minstrelsy Ancient and Modern*. In it he included one called 'Bonnie Susie Cleland', the repeated refrain of which runs, 'And bonnie Susie Cleland is to be burnt in Dundee!' The ballad tells how the lass refuses to give up her English lover, so her father ties her to the stake, her brother piles up the bonfire, and the family burn her alive. There is no mention of witchcraft in the ballad, and Motherwell, who personally collected the piece, had no idea how old it was. There may be no relation to the Dundee witchcraft executions, but I include it for interest's sake.

Charms and charming at the Kirk Sessions

As noted in the previous story, most cases of magical misdemeanour did not attract capital punishment. The Kirk Session records of the various parishes around Dundee are full of the kind of beliefs and practices that ministers were dealing with on a regular basis. For instance, in May 1652 Mrs Robertson from Bonniton confessed to the Auchterhouse Kirk Session that she had taken her sick daughter to the Kirkton well and washed the child's eyes while saying: 'Fish beare fin and fulle beare gall, All ye ill of my bairn's eyen in ye wall fall.' The charm was clearly meant to transfer the malady to the water applied to the eyes by a process of sympathetic magic. The Kirkton Well, also known as the Lady Well because before the Reformation it had been dedicated to the Virgin Mary, was a well-known healing well much resorted to by charmers. In punishment Mrs Robertson and Janet Fyffe, who had taught her the charm, were ordered to sit on the stool of repentance in sackcloth in front of the whole congregation, and publicly apologise for their error. This Janet Fyffe did, but her companion could not keep the appointment: 'whereas Mrs Robertson should have done the same, it pleased the Lord before that time to call upon her by death.'

At a time when being suspected of witchcraft could lead to imprisonment or worse, people were understandably keen to preserve their good reputation, so Kirk Sessions also dealt with false accusations of witchcraft. For example, in 1696 Jean Morom had to apologise on her knees to Jean Anderson in Longforgan for calling her a witch, and, in 1646, Isabel Gall complained to the Auchterhouse Session about Janet Thomson, whom she said had slandered her with the name witch. Janet Thomson was a servant and seems to have been a quarrelsome individual, being frequently rebuked by the Session for slandering others.

A tombstone from Auchterhouse, with the Angels of the Resurrection deafening a skeleton with their trumpets. (*Ségolene Dupuy*)

Kirkton of Auchterhouse. A datestone from the church of 1630 is embedded in the walls of the present church. *(Geoff Holder)*

The pre-Reformation church at Monifieth. *(Perth & Kinross Libraries)*

It was a similar story elsewhere. In November 1628 a poor woman named Bessie Archer confessed to the Monifieth Session to using charms for the past seven years. She was ordered to make repentance in sackcloth and was warned she would be severely punished if found charming again. In 1629 Agnes Meldrum was excommunicated by the same Session for charming; excommunication not only imperilled your immortal soul, it also prevented anyone in the parish sheltering or doing business with you, so Agnes, who had been resisting the Session for weeks, quickly apologised for the charming, and was readmitted to the congregation after appearing in sackcloth at the front of the church.

The minutes of the Auchterhouse Session also reveal just how obsessed the Presbyterian Church was with witchcraft. On 5 July 1646, a penitential fast was ordered 'because of the frequent scandal of witches and charmers in this part of the land.' On 6 January 1650, 'the minister desired the session to make search everywhere in their own quarters if they knew of any witches or charmers in the parish, and delate them to the next session.' And on 14 November of the same year, another penitential fast was kept for several reasons, among them the ongoing evils of witches and charmers in the land, and a fervent hope 'that the Lord would discover here all the work of Satan as he has begun to do in other places of the land, and bless all means that are and shall be for that effect.'

Some late examples of witch belief

Witchcraft ceased to be a capital crime in 1735 – in fact the Witchcraft Act of that year specifically stated that witchcraft *did not exist* and anyone claiming to have supernatural powers was in fact a charlatan. This did not mean that people stopped believing in witchcraft of course; the beliefs mutated into superstitions, prejudices and eventually stories told around the fire, but at least any woman who fitted the witch stereotype no longer had to worry about being tortured and executed. Still, the old beliefs retained some of their power into the century of progress and science.

In 1825 a cat became the constant companion of a night watchman on Tay Street, keeping pace with his patrol, pausing when he paused, and generally imitating his actions. The sagacious animal attracted some attention, with people turning out in the early hours to see it. According to the report in the *Courier* for 7 April, several witnesses came away convinced the cat was a witch. And in 1871 a little boy in Dundee was afflicted with a sore upon his right leg, the injury threatening his ability to walk. Doctors could do nothing, but an old Irish woman claimed she could cure the sore by the 'gold-touch'. What happened next was described in *The Mysteries of All Nations* by James Grant:

> She asked for and obtained the marriage ring of the invalid's mother. With the ring the strange woman rubbed three times round the sore. She performed the same operation next day, and on the next again. On the fourth day no mark of a sore could be discovered. No doubt remained on the parents' and neighbours' minds that the operator was a white witch, possessed of valuable charms.

But the best example of a nineteenth-century witch was given in the *Courier* in September 1828. Elspeth Gilruth of Whale Lane had developed a local reputation for witchery. When a new brig, the *Mary*, failed to launch from the New Ship Building Co.'s yard, the shipwrights blamed a minor engineering issue. But many on the docks remembered that Elspeth had argued with one of the brig's owners about the size or quality of some seamen's stocking she had knitted, the dispute ending with Elspeth muttering curses against the new vessel. Accordingly one of the other shipowners decided a show of conciliation was in order, so Elspeth was invited to the dinner intended to celebrate the launch.

> Bare-headed, a deputation waited upon the agent of Satan, who condescended to honour them with her company. Elspeth was placed at the head of the table, and showed, by the justice which she did to the good cheer, that the devil's service had not deprived her of an appetite.

Dock Street as Elspeth Gilruth would have known it in the early nineteenth century. *(Perth & Kinross Libraries)*

Having eaten and drunk her fill, the rather self-satisfied woman was escorted home with an extensive doggy-bag and the gift of a gold sovereign. Early the next day a second launch was attempted, and, of course, all went smoothly. You've got to keep the witch on your side.

Helen Duncan

Although not a witch, Helen Duncan was the last person to be imprisoned (but not the last to be prosecuted) under the 1735 Witchcraft Act, which actually was directed against those who claimed to have psychic or magical powers – powers the law assumed were illusory. Born in Callander in Perthshire, from 1912 Duncan lived in Dundee for much of her early adult life, working in a jute mill, Dundee Royal Infirmary and a bleach factory. At the same time she was building up a national reputation as one of the most impressive mediums of her time, giving 'sittings' all over the country. She was lauded by spiritualists and investigated – to an extent – by researchers, convicted of fraud in 1933, and, when living in Portsmouth during the Second World War, was famously sentenced to nine months' imprisonment in 1944 for allegedly communicating with sailors whose deaths (and the sinking of their ships) had not been officially released. She died in 1956.

Duncan started giving séances in the family home in the 1920s, encouraged by her husband Henry, an ardent spiritualist, who became her promoter and champion. In post-First World War Dundee there was a huge appetite for the comfort provided by an apparent talk with the recently dead, and Duncan's abilities to communicate with the Other Side – facilitated by her spirit guides 'Dr Williams' and 'Albert' – made her much in demand. Soon she was supplementing, then exclusively providing, the family income, moving on to live in Edinburgh and later London.

It is probably accurate to say that Helen Duncan is as controversial now as she was during her lifetime. At the extremes, some see her as a clever fraud preying on the bereaved, while her supporters regard her as a misunderstood martyr who was genuinely in contact with the dead. These views, and others, are hotly debated in books, websites and the pages of the *Journal of the Society for Psychical Research*. Duncan was a physical medium, supposedly generating spirit forms using an etheric substance called ectoplasm. The psychic investigator Harry Price was convinced her 'ectoplasm' was simply regurgitated cheesecloth, egg-whites, surgical gauze and other substances Duncan had swallowed before the séance, and certainly photographs of Duncan's spirit beings appear to be composed of clumsy drapes of muslin-like cloth and embarrassing childish masks and rubber gloves. On the other hand, there were many examples of sittings where Duncan seemed to know information about the sitter that could not easily have been gained – such as when visitors turned up impromptu, allowing no time for research or devious tricks.

Probably the best book on Helen Duncan is *Hellish Nell* by the historian Malcolm Gaskell. Digging deep into the archives and the testimonies of attendees at séances, Gaskill shows how the seventeen-stone medium consistently used crude and mundane methods of deception, frauds that the faith of her supporters simply overlooked or found ways to justify. It is possible that Duncan had genuine powers, but that they were too unreliable or mercurial to depend on when it came to the crunch – that is, when performing in a séance for money (hence the frauds). So complex and contradictory is the evidence for and against her that, in the end, the answer to the question of whether Helen Duncan was truly in touch with the dead may come down to one thing – your own beliefs.

two

WATCH THE SKIES! UFOS AND SIMILAR STRANGENESS

UFOs and IFOs (Identified Flying Objects)

Long before the terms 'flying saucer' or UFO (unidentified flying object) were coined in the late 1940s, people have been seeing strange things in the sky over Dundee. Under the heading 'Strange phenomenon' the *Advertiser* for 22 December 1882 described a curious sighting:

> Yesterday forenoon, between ten and eleven o'clock, the attention of several persons in Broughty Ferry was directed for a time to a somewhat unusual sight in the heavens. The sun at the same time was shining brightly, being about due south, when a star was seen in close proximity to it. The star was a little above the sun's path, and the peculiar phenomenon was seen by various persons, who had their attention directed to it. Being daytime, the star did not have the brilliant luminous radiance stars exhibit at night, but was of a milky white appearance, and seemed, when seen through a glass, to be of a crescent shape. Being on a light blue ground, and lying between two white clouds, it was seen to great advantage.

A second report in the same paper on 25 December entitled 'The peculiar phenomenon in the heavens' – noted the same 'unknown luminous body' was also seen by several witnesses in Dundee.

The sighting was subsequently explained as being either Venus or Mercury, the two planets between us and the sun, but contradictory claims were put forward, stating that Venus was in a different part of the sky that day, and Mercury was too close to the sun to be visible on that day. Another suggestion was that it was a supernova briefly flaring up, but in that case it would probably have been spotted by others around the world. In the end the most likely clue is not in the object's position in the sky – which can be easily mistaken – but its 'crescent shape' as seen through a telescope. This almost certainly identifies it as Venus, as the planet was showing as a crescent in telescopes elsewhere around this time.

Rather more mundane was a bright light seen off the east coast on the early morning of 16 December 1881. The *Morning Post* described how the evening before a fire-balloon had been sent up from Monifieth, 'which had been carried along the coast by a gentle breeze, and, after burning all night, extinguished and collapsed off Montrose.' The fire-balloon origin for the strange light was echoed over a century later when the *Courier* for 17 September 2007 described several witnesses spotting 'a series of eerie lights drifting silently towards Broughty Ferry'. In total eight glowing orange objects were seen. Their source, it turned out, was the fiftieth anniversary party hosted by a Dundee hairdressing salon. Family, friends and staff past and present of Jaconelli's salon had gathered at the West Park Centre on Perth Road and as part of the celebrations released Chinese lanterns into the night sky. Also known as Thai lanterns or fire lanterns, these are fragile paper globes surrounding a wire frame and a small burning flame; as the air inside the globe heats up the ephemeral structures float for as long as the flame burns. 'We called the airport last night to make sure we were able to release the lanterns, and they put us in touch with air traffic control,' explained Doreen Jaconelli. 'People put their wish inside and then we lit them and let them go – we can't believe people thought they might have been UFOs!' In fact, since the mid-2000s, dozens if not hundreds of sightings of supposed 'UFOs' nationwide have been caused by the release of the orange glowing lanterns – there was another spate in Dundee during the 2009 Christmas/New Year period, when dozens of readers – including a councillor – contacted the *Courier* with reports of silent, orange lights in the sky. Just as interesting, at least six other people then got in touch, saying they had released Chinese lanterns during the holidays.

Similar confusion can be caused by the irresponsible release of flares, which are meant to be used only in times of distress. Numerous witnesses reported a low-moving, very bright red and yellow light above Whitfield and Baldovie on the night of 1 September 1980. After being visible for several minutes it turned white and disappeared. An account in the *Courier* on 3 September, however, identified the cause: 'It was a Verey light or a flare falling steadily and drifting from west to east. It left a trail of smoke and changed to white when it was burning out.'

On several occasions Dundonians have had a grand view as meteors or spacecraft debris have spectacularly burned up as they entered the atmosphere (all the following reports are from the *Courier* or the *Evening Telegraph*, usually from the day after the sighting). A fast-moving grey object with flames coming from the rear was seen by many between 6.45 and 7 a.m. on 14 October 1982. On 4 August 1983 a 'bluish object surrounded by red with a white tail' was seen to fall for about a minute around 10.30 p.m. by several witnesses. Another fireball streaked across the skies just before midnight on 28 July 1995, variously described by the numerous witnesses as 'a bright blue ball,' 'red', 'blue-green,' and 'a big glowing ball with a long tail.' One man likened it to a speeding rocket, while other comments compared the sight to a flash of lightning. Several people saw more than one light, which is common when a meteor breaks up. Interestingly, in this case the majority of witnesses thought they were definitely seeing a meteor, with very few opting for the spacecraft option.

Often sightings of UFOs are actually of modern aerial or space technology. On 18 January 1979 the *Courier* reported the experience of five people who had seen something strange on Whitfield Avenue. 'It was a weird metallic-looking object with a length of smoke coming out of the back,' said a witness. 'Although it was very high up, none of us could see the smoke at the rear stretch or tail off. It just seemed to remain the same length.' A spokesman at RAF Leuchars suggested this was probably an aircraft venting fuel, a procedure undertaken when a pilot decides the jet is carrying too much fuel for a particular manoeuvre. The release of the fuel can create a smoke-like effect from the rear of the tanks. And indeed a military plane was flying over the area just north of Dundee at the time of the sighting. Another example of modern technology was responsible for reports from May 2001 and August 2002 of 'rings' drifting into each other and moving up and down – these were in fact laser displays from an entertainment event.

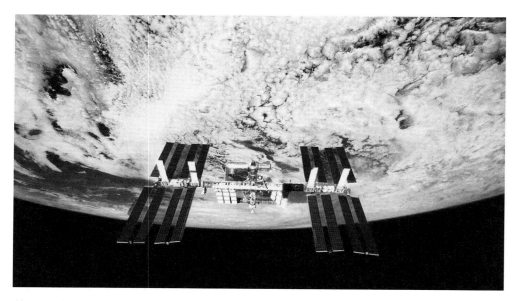

The International Space Station, the likely source for many UFO sightings. *(NASA)*

What these cases illustrate is that, despite tabloid hysteria over 'alien encounters' or 'invasion from space', most strange things seen in the sky are very probably either the result of natural factors (the planet Venus, the star Sirius, meteors, birds, lenticular clouds, unusual solar phenomena, atmospheric conditions and so on) or man-made artifacts (helicopters, aeroplanes, satellites, hot-air or weather balloons, spacecraft debris, fire lanterns and such like). One of the most common sources of excitement among UFO buffs in Dundee is a large white light that is seen traveling in straight or curved lines but is much brighter than most satellites. This is in fact the International Space Station (ISS), which, after the Moon, is the brightest object in the night sky. The ISS has been continuously occupied since November 2000, and was being constructed in space for years before that. It completes its orbit sixteen times a day, and is often at it brightest in the time after sundown or before dawn (because it is so high – 250 miles up – it reflects the sun that is below the horizon at ground level). The NASA website has a page that allows you to work out when the ISS will next be visible from your location.

One of the great figures of paranormal research, John A. Keel (author of *The Mothman Prophecies* among other works), coined the acronym LITS – Lights In The Sky. And, indeed, the typical UFO sighting is really a LITS event, with no description of an actual structured craft or anything else beyond just 'a light in the sky'. To pick a few examples from many recorded by the *Courier*: seven men in a fitting shop in Arbroath saw a 'bright cigar-shaped object' hovering above the Bell Rock in the early hours of 24 January 1979; a fruitpicker witnessed two large motionless bright lights at 9.22 p.m. above Drumgeith Road on 22 August 1979; a big red light with 'flashing red and white lights round the edge' was seen over Whitfield at about 6.50 p.m. on 6 December 1979; several witnesses reported a 'bright semi-circular light' from Gauldry on 19 September 1980, with another event the same evening when two children saw bright white lights 'like stars' over the Midmill area; and two men at Booker Cash and Carry on the Kingsway spotted a bright white light in the sky which 'suddenly vanished' above Newburgh at

8.30 a.m. on 25 October 1996. In none of these cases was anything more unusual than a 'bright light' reported, and most if not all will have very ordinary causes. Some sightings, however, cannot be so easily tidied away, and the few sightings that follow are truly strange.

The police sighting of 1980

Sightings involving police officers always attract special attention, as it is assumed the descriptions given in these cases will be reliable and accurate. There is also the added bonus – for UFO investigators at least – that police involvement adds status, even glamour, to the case. So when an off-duty policeman spotted a UFO from his home in the Gowrie Park housing estate on Sunday, 30 March 1980, people paid attention. The officer was awakened by a 'hollow metal hum' similar to the 'amplified sound of a child's spinning top.' He got up and from his north-west facing bedroom window saw some dull lights moving slowly in a diamond formation over the Carse of Gowrie. 'There was a full or almost full moon and it looked as though the light was reflecting off four objects,' the officer told the *Courier* on 31 March. He estimated they were about three-quarters of a mile away, and seemed metallic. 'They appeared to stop at one point and hover over the Star Inn Road, near Benvie.' During this time the strange noise had been getting louder, but at this point it reduced in volume, and so the officer thought he might have been imagining things and went back to bed. But then the noise returned, even louder, and so he returned to the window and saw one of the lights coming down to the ground. 'It descended like a lift – there was no shape, just a glow,' he said. 'At ground level it just disappeared, but there were noises from where it came down. For a time the noise seemed to intensify. When I looked for the other three lights they had disappeared.'

Was this a 'landing'? The sighting lasted for around thirty minutes, and apart from the original witness's report, there are several corroborative details. Clearly something unusual was going on, so on-duty police officers were summoned. The first policeman on the scene said he too had heard the strange noises when he first arrived, and two other officers in a car appeared to have seen one or more of the lights. A full search of the area found nothing, but two milk boys who were interviewed in Menzieshill both reported hearing similar sounds, and an anonymous caller to Dundee police headquarters said he had heard 'buzzing-cum-whooshing' noises from Menzieshill at the same time as the initial sighting. The degree and volume of noises reported by these several witnesses is relatively unusual for UFO sightings.

All this suggests *something* took place in the early hours of that Sunday morning, but what it was is hard to say. RAF Leuchars confirmed there was no air traffic in the area at the time. It could have been a private helicopter, or some kind of covert military training exercise, or criminal activity. Or it could be an entirely unexplained event.

As is often the case, once a sighting is reported in the press, other people become sufficiently emboldened to come forward with their experiences. Consequently the *Courier* for the next day had two UFO stories. In the first, a man in Baldovie said he saw a shining object low in the sky on Wednesday 26 March, at about 6 p.m. Something was hanging from the object, giving it an impression of a balloon or parachute. 'It stopped slightly north of Baldovie for about twenty minutes,' he said, 'before moving off in an easterly direction and eventually rising out of sight.' And another off-duty policeman reported seeing a 'rugby ball shaped' object near Forfar on the evening of Saturday 29 March. The officer estimated the 'hovering or floating' object was some two or three miles away, and had a white top and a glowing orange base – which suggests it was a hot-air balloon, the orange being the burner at the base. Although both reports appeared on 1 April, there is nothing obvious within them to suggest they were newspaper hoaxes; however, both sightings seem to have clearly mundane origins, and it appears someone was flying a balloon around the Dundee/Angus area that week.

A second police sighting

The witness in this case was a retired police sergeant, and the details are truly extraordinary. The sighting was reported to the Anglo-Scottish UFO Research Association (ASUFORA), which, during its short lifespan – 2002 to 2004 – collected a number of interesting UFO stories. I am grateful to Steve Hammond, who used to run the ASUFORA website, for sharing these stories with me. ASUFORA put great emphasis on the confidentiality of their reporting forum, so that witnesses were not identified, and this has been respected here.

The retired officer was looking south towards Craigowl Hill, which is topped with communications masts and overlooks Balluderon stone circle (described in chapter five). It was an early afternoon in 1992 or 1993. His eye was caught by something strange in the clouds – 'It seemed as if part of the cloud was travelling in the opposite direction to the rest,' he wrote in his witness report. Slowly he worked out that what he was seeing was an otherwise invisible sphere whose presence was only revealed because the clouds passing behind it outlined its shape. It was 'like a glass globe having smoke blown over it in a wind tunnel, invisible, until it was shown up by smoke passing over it.' This invisible, stationary, perfect sphere was 'docked' to the radio masts at the top of the hill, like a Zeppelin attached to its docking mast. The comparison with the masts allowed an approximation of its size – 50 to 100ft in diameter. After perhaps two minutes the object turned clockwise on its own axis and smoothly shifted

The communications masts on Craigowl Hill; a UFO was seen 'docking' here. In the foreground is Balluderon stone circle. (*Geoff Holder*)

from a sphere to an oval in shape, before making a 'very rapid downwards movement' and following the contours of the far side of the hill until it went out of sight. Its exit was silent, without light or smoke, and the movement was 'instant' with no acceleration, a manouevre impossible for an aircraft. 'In fact,' finished the retired officer, 'it looked as though it should have driven itself into the ground, the speed it was travelling.'

The incident was reported a decade after it happened, and the workings of memory may have reconfigured some details. But if even some elements are accurate, this is a genuinely strange sighting; the only parallels I can think of are 'invisible' UFOs that have been occasionally reported in the environment around US military bases.

The Golden Sphere

Another sighting from the ASUFORA files took place on a slightly cloudy Sunday on 6 August 2000, when a Dundee couple watched a 'small gold sphere' behaving strangely over the mouth of the Tay. For a number of minutes it remained stationary at an estimated height of between 4,000 to 8,000ft, giving the impression to the witnesses that it was 'observing' the RAF base at Leuchars about five miles away. During the next twenty-five minutes the sphere 'zig-zagged three times then dropped about 1,000ft then shot upwards and disappeared at a fantastic speed.' If this behaviour was accurately described then whatever it was could clearly not have been a conventional aircraft or balloon. The report is quite detailed but there are a few curious elements – for example, the man thought the object was ten to fifteen miles from his position, and estimated its size to be three to 6ft in diameter, whereas for an object to be visible at that distance it must be several metres across at least. It is also possible the distance distorted the witnesses' perception of how the object behaved. Nevertheless, this remains an unexplained incident.

The Orchar Park incident

Possibly the most dramatic Dundee UFO sighting took place on the evening of 20 February 1996. Three twelve-year-olds were so terrified at what they saw in Orchar Park, Broughty Ferry, that they arrived home crying and in a 'distraught, hysterical state,' according to the mother of one of them. Pamela Stewart described how her son Cameron, along with his friends Joanne Leach and Graham Binnie, all pupils at Grove Academy, came belting into her house just after 7.30 p.m., all in a terrible state and speaking at once about something awful they had seen in the park. Mrs Stewart calmed the youngsters down and got them to describe clearly what they had witnessed. They all described a 'burger' shaped craft, with domes shaped like the pointed ends of a rugby ball on the upper and lower surfaces. There was a band of both static and flickering red and blue lights round the middle, the white light being the most intense. The silent craft moved towards the children and shone three triangular lights at them. Not surprisingly, they panicked and ran home to Ramsay Street, thinking it was following them. The last view they had of the object was as it was heading over towards the Bughties, north of Monifieth Road.

Mrs Stewart got the trio to each separately draw a picture of what they had seen, and the images were apparently remarkably consistent. The children were featured in the *Courier* on 21 February and again the following day. The paper contacted RAF Leuchars, which stated

Looking north from Orchar Park, Broughty Ferry. The UFO sighted by the three children moved in this direction. *(Geoff Holder)*

there had been some night flying at the time, but there was nothing that fitted the descriptions, and no radar traces from air traffic control. The staff at Mills Observatory were equally baffled.

The children's experience took place on the Tuesday evening and was in the local paper the following morning. As has been mentioned before, 'live stories' in the press often generate their own momentum, with two results – firstly, other people come forward with their individual experiences, and secondly journalists are more willing to pay attention to them because the subject is 'hot'. So on the Wednesday the *Courier* also gave space to a family in Dryburgh Street who claimed to have videoed a 'flashing light' in the sky between 8.45 and 10 p.m. the previous evening. Although initially this might seem to have supported the Orchar Park sighting, Brian Kelly of Mills Observatory viewed the shaky footage and concluded it was a case of mistaken identity, the light simply being the bright star Sirius (Sirius is mistaken for a UFO surprisingly often).

The following day, Thursday 22 February, there were more stories, although none had very convincing details. A nine-year-old Broughty Ferry boy claimed to have seen a moving object 'like a rugby ball with lights on it' over the Esplanade on 13 February. It was about 'five lampposts away and bigger than the moon.' This sounds so close to the Orchar Park description it may have been influenced by the newspaper reports. A woman driving along Lawside Road towards Dundee Royal Infirmary with her fifteen-year-old granddaughter saw something heading overhead from east to west at about 8.15 p.m. on the 20th. Some children in Broughty Ferry thought they may have seen something on the same evening, but no details were given. And nine-year-old Stacey Traynor, along with three friends, saw something strange near Dryburgh Primary School at about 6.30 p.m. on 14 February. 'It was like a bright, white light,' said Stacey, 'and it had wings and a red tail-like bit at the back which was flashing.' It has to be said that this sounds very much like some kind of aeroplane…

The Lochee Lights

What was also possibly an aircraft alarmed two teenagers walking along Blackhill Road near Lochee Park on Wednesday, 3 March 1982. The pair, who were fifth-year pupils at Menziehill High School, told the *Courier* two days later that they saw a 'semi-circular, and very, very bright' object descend slowly from about 100ft in the air to a patch of sloping ground behind the gardens of Ancrum Drive. They couldn't tell if it actually landed on the slope or hovered just above the ground; after remaining in the spot for five minutes it took off again, and headed towards the east of the city, showing a red light. The sighting took place at 7.15 p.m., and that evening RAF Leuchars logged a call from someone reporting a UFO over Dundee, presumably the same craft. Now, I was once in a small helicopter when the pilot noticed a door was not fully closed; he promptly landed on the first available piece of open ground, secured the door, and took off again, all in about three minutes – and anyone observing from a distance may have been puzzled by our actions. On first glance the pupils' sighting sounds very much like a description of a helicopter that landed to briefly fix a similar minor problem. There are, however, two strange aspects to the episode. The first is that the waste ground was sloping, hardly an ideal landing spot for a helicopter. And secondly, despite the students managing to approach within 50 to 100ft – until their view was blocked by the wall beside the tennis courts – they did not hear a single sound; and the noise of a helicopter landing and taking off is hard to miss.

'The UFOs are back!' shouted the *Courier*'s headline some months later. Late on the night of 4 July the paper was contacted by several callers from the Lochee and surrounding area, all reporting a strange object in the sky that was visible for several minutes. It was variously described as being 'saucer-shaped,' 'about the size of a large plane, but its shape was round,' possessing 'orange and yellow flashing lights' and 'moving too fast for an ordinary aircraft'. A spokesman at RAF Leuchars commented that it was almost certainly a communications satellite. One curious element was added in the paper on 6 July – many residents of Hazlehead Court in Ardler were disturbed by 'a loud whistling and buzzing noise' between 11 p.m. and midnight, the time the Lochee sightings were reported. Many people came out of their houses in an attempt to trace the source of the noise, and, having later read the UFO reports in the *Courier*, some wondered if there was a connection.

The Fissiparous Sphere

Even stranger was an incident on 24 July 1993, when a blinding white light was seen over Dundee at 10.30 p.m. The spherical object glowed with a 'strange intensity' as it hovered 100ft above the ground, then began to rise up before the brilliance became muted and the thing split first into two, and then into two groups of three to four white lights. Up to now the description sounds as though it might have been an elaborate firework, but this is disproved by what happened next, because the various parts shot off in different directions, one towards Invergowrie, another on the way to Falkland, both elements travelling in straight lines. The oddity was witnessed by a man who contacted the Ministry of Defence, receiving little in the way of a satisfactory answer for his pains; it was later included in the wholesale release of MoD UFO files in 2008-2009.

Rough diamond

A curious case was reported on the UFOScotland website by researchers Allan Robertson and Jeannie McKay. The unnamed witness was a driving instructor who, along with his seventeen-year-old pupil, saw a black diamond-shaped craft from Fairmuir Park. At this point it was moving north. Some twenty or so minutes later, as the driving lesson continued, both witnesses again spotted the craft, 'hovering high in the sky and glowing like a star,' possibly above the general area of the Dryburgh Estate. After about a minute it rotated anti-clockwise through 360 degrees and briefly sent down an orange beam of light which then returned back to the underside of the craft – 'like a row of Christmas lights coming on one after the other in sequence, first down from the craft, then back up towards it.' The beam did not come all the way down, descending for perhaps a quarter of the height between the UFO and the ground over around two or three seconds, 'pausing' for the same period, and then taking the same time to go back up. Shortly afterwards the object moved off to the southwest and instructor and pupil followed it for ten minutes in the car until it passed over Invergowrie Bay and across the Tay into Fife.

The instructor gave a detailed description of the craft, which he said was round or perhaps slightly oval, although he definitely said it was diamond-shaped (perhaps it was a diamond from below, but had a curved upper surface). It lacked any of the lights found on conventional aircraft, and in motion glowed a bright white or slightly yellowish colour. It travelled along the shorter axis of the 'diamond', that is, the longer axis stuck out like wings. Speed was hard to estimate, although it may have been around 60mph.

The sighting took place at around 6.20 p.m. on Wednesday, 27 January 1999, lasting until approximately 7 p.m. Two days later the driving instructor found out that one of his relatives, along with her nine- and thirteen-year-old daughters, had had their own experience on the morning of 28 January. Neither mother nor daughters had heard of the instructor's sighting. He was convinced they had seen the same UFO as he had, but it seems to me there are not enough points in common between the two sightings to make a positive match.

They had been in a car travelling south down Thomson Street at 8.40 a.m. when all three saw a very bright white or yellowish 'shooting star' over the Tay, in the general direction of the Tay Rail Bridge. 'It was hovering over the water with two yellow beams coming from underneath.' It slowly started to rise vertically, then sped up. At this point they lost sight of it because of the height of the buildings. By the time they turned into Magdalen Yard Road and had a clear view of the Tay, the object had vanished. Thomson Street is a narrow steeply-sloping road which looks onto the river and the railway bridge, but which has limited views of the river. These two sightings may or may not have been related: but what were they? The Thomson Street case could possibly have been a reflection (reflections account for a surprising number of UFO sightings, especially in moving vehicles) but the extended sighting the previous evening is a real poser.

The Cloudship

A detailed sighting from 27 December 1998 appeared in the *Courier* for 4 February 2000, prompted by the spate of reports in January of that year. An anonymous Monifieth resident described how she was making breakfast around 9 a.m. when she saw an 'enormous edifice' stationary in the sky about half a mile away and 500ft up. The sand-coloured object resembled two woks placed together rim to rim, and may have been 40ft high. After it was briefly obscured by clouds, the structure reappeared, this time displaying three windows in its upper surface, which now had the appearance of highly polished steel. The woman got the impression the clouds actually turned into the craft, or had been manufactured by the ship as a form of concealment (many readers will no doubt remember the film *Independence Day*, in which the invading alien spacecraft did exactly the same; perhaps significantly, the film was a big hit in the UK two years before this sighting). After about seven minutes of remaining static, the object began climbing and moving south amid a wash of green light, the perspective changing so that the upper 'wok' 'was like a volcano with two tyre-like curves going round it and a shadow as if the top of the cone was concave.' Soon it became a speck in the sky, then after a brief pause changed course from southwest to northwest, leaving a triple vapour trail behind.

The Monifieth Fireball

A huge orange fireball appeared over Monifieth around 9.30 p.m. on 27 July 1999. It was, as Jennifer Young explained to the *Courier* two days later, 'straight out of *The X-Files.*' First moving in a northerly direction, towards Forfar, the object suddenly stopped, changed direction, and split into two vertical, parallel lines, before morphing into 'a kind of question mark, without the dot.' A friend of Jennifer's in Monikie had also seen the same thing, and there was a brief contemporaneous report of a person in Tayport seeing an unusual coloured shape over Dundee. A member of staff at the St Andrews Observatory offered a possible explanation: a fighter jet flying at high altitude. In some circumstances the jet creates vapour crystals that give the appearance of a fireball, while the parallel lines could have been caused by the wing trails, which alter shape as the plane changes direction and then remain behind as the plane moves on, to be blown into other shapes by the wind.

'Have grey aliens stolen the brains of Dundee?'

That was the headline in the *Daily Mail* for 3 March 1997. The paper's sarcastic ire was directed at 'more than a dozen' Dundonians who rang an alien abduction helpline, claiming they had been beamed up to extraterrestrial craft where the 'Greys' had 'fed on information from their brains.' The helpline was run by thirty-eight-year-old psychic counsellor, Graham Wylie from Auchterhouse. Mr Wylie was quoted as saying: 'The Greys' mother ship is coming to earth in the next three or four years and our government knows all about it. I expect them to make an announcement later this year.' Further, the alien race, whose home planet was thirty-seven light years away, would arrive in force by the year 2000. As neither of these events have, as far as can be determined, taken place, there is the inevitable tendency to look back in amusement. But context helps a great deal in understanding what was going on. For 1997 was slap bang in the middle of what can be described as 'the *X-Files* effect'.

For around seven years from its debut in 1993, *The X-Files* was one of the key players in global popular culture. The television series, and its accompanying films, set out an irresistible mythos: the aliens were here, and not only did our governments know, they were in league with them. The series brought the various disparate shards of counter-cultural and sub-cultural dissonance into sharp relief. Subjects such as conspiracy theories, extraterrestrial visitation, supernatural entities, alien abduction, secret élites and inexplicably advanced technology – all previously the province of fringe groups – suddenly became mainstream fare. And it seemed our collective imagination was suddenly set on fire. The result was a worldwide explosion in all things paranormal and conspiratorial. UFO sightings and UFO groups mushroomed. Self-confessed alien abductees came forward to be interviewed on television. Books, websites and conferences dedicated to UFOs and conspiracies became an ever-expanding area. After a good run *The X-Files* itself ceased to captivate audiences from around 2001, and so we can now gain some perspective on the show's incredible impact. It clearly tapped into the zeitgeist, particularly a profound distrust that many people felt about the secrecy and agendas of governments and military forces – not to mention covert bodies such as alleged 'secret rulers of the world'. It was also millennial, in that it consistently signposted the coming apocalypse – or, at least, the end of the world as we know it (because the aliens were coming to get us). To an extent, it was a kind of mania, and many people were caught up in the slipstream.

Graham Wylie's abduction counselling group was just one of similar bodies that sprung up around the world. More about the abduction helpline was included in a flyer he distributed in 1997-98, offering: 'Telephone and written contact. Physical and psychic protection possible. Counselling and advice. Distant and personal healing. Vetted abductee support network.' Wylie described himself as a psychic channeller and healer who obtained his powers and knowledge from a space being called Josef of Aragon, who was a member of the Council Of Nine and head of one of the twenty-four planetary civilizations. It was Josef who extended physical and psychic protection to people, thus defending them from alien abduction or psychic interference by the Greys.

The X-Files effect was an example of 'cultural tracking,' the phrase ufologists use to describe how themes, events and notions in popular culture both *reflect* our contemporary fears, concerns and obsessions, and *reinforce* them, even *changing* them so that fiction becomes reality. So, for example, in the 1950s and '60s, when 'flying saucers' was a buzzword that sold millions of books and prompted hippie-era groups such as Jefferson Airplane to write anthems with titles like 'Have You Seen The Saucers?', the standard UFO sighting was of a discoid craft. In that era, if something strange was seen in the sky, it was almost always described as a saucer or disc. These days, however, 'flying saucers' as a phrase has fallen out of fashion, and very few sightings use this description (the current fashion is for black triangles or diamond shapes, which partly relates to the exposure this UFO-form had in *The X-Files*). Again, Steven Spielberg's 1979 film *Close Encounters of the Third Kind* was massively influential on our collective imagination, prompting not only a great surge in UFO sightings, but also a solidification of ideas about *what UFOs looked like*. Changes in pop-culture fashion also seep into the style of newspaper journalism, so that reports from the 1960s typically talk about 'little green men from Mars,' post-Spielberg 1979-era accounts usually use the phrase 'close encounters', and mid-1990s pieces almost inevitably referred back to *The X-Files'* protagonists, lazily describing local UFO enthusiasts as 'like a real-life Mulder and Scully.'

The impact of the film *Independence Day* has already been mentioned, while the movies *Fire in The Sky* and *Communion* (the latter based on Whitley Streiber's best-selling book) popularised not only the *idea* of alien abduction, but also the *form it supposedly took*. In the old, fringe days of ufology, accounts of abduction experiences in the UFO magazines were varied and diverse; but as soon as the 'alien abduction' theme went mainstream, accounts became more-or-less the same, following a stereotyped pattern that reflected the 'master-narrative' set out in popular films and television. In another trope, the rave, dance and festival counterculture of the early 1990s adopted the 'Grey' alien face as the digital age's equivalent of the pirate flag, a marker of anti-authoritarian, free-thinking and fun-loving dissidence; and whereas once extraterrestrial lifeforms were described in a bewildering variety of shapes and sizes by those who said they had encountered them, the 'Grey' form is now universal. These days the principal transmission for UFO-memes is the internet, where both hardcore enthusiasts and casual visitors swap tales of the ongoing extraterrestrial threat, and YouTube hosts dodgy (and usually misidentified) 'UFO' video clips.

Since the terrorist attacks of 9/11, however, we seem to have collectively refocused our demonology, and alien abductions, although still claimed to occur, are no longer the stuff of headlines; and so it appears there are no longer Dundonians seeking to receive anti-alien psychic help or protection from the bodysnatching Greys.

Millennium sightings

Another UFO 'flap' occurred in the press in late 1999 and the early part of 2000. The *Courier* for 28 and 29 January included several sightings. The first was around 8.30 a.m. on 17 December, when Michael Clark spotted three bright white lights from the patio of Liff Hospital. They were travelling extremely slowly over the Tay but then the leading light seemed to break away and split into four parts. There was no noise during the sighting, which lasted for about ten minutes. At 8 p.m. sometime in early January, a man saw 'a solid ball of white light' moving low in the sky over Duncan of Jordanstone College of Art, which sounds like he had seen the International Space Station. On 25 January several separate witnesses saw something strange in the sky just after 7 a.m. The most common description was of a brightly coloured object flashing orange and blue, travelling at great speed south over the Tay (this may have been a meteor or space debris burning up). Then, on the following day, a man on Ancrum Road spotted a mysterious light with a smoky trail descending over the Law at about 10.30 p.m., a sighting later confirmed by two people on Brantwood Avenue. The intensity of the orange glow, the smoky trail and the slow-moving nature of the light made the police suspect someone had let off a flare.

Star Trekking

In one respect, however, extraterrestrials can definitely be said to be walking among us. For Vulcans, Romulans, Izarians and other alien races regularly turn up in the amateur films made by a Dundee group of *Star Trek* fans. So far the adventures of the *Starship Intrepid* have encompassed a pair of feature-length films and two shorts, all available for free on the internet at www.starshipintrepid.net. Along with sites in Dundee, intergalactic settings have been simulated by locations in Glen Doll, Dunkeld and Arbroath's Abbey Theatre, and the productions come with a full complement of costumes, weapons and alien make-up. The zero-budget movies typically involve a cast and technical crew of thirty, and such is the enthusiasm that *Trek*-fans have for the science fiction colossus, that the Dundee team regularly receive assistance from fans in Europe and the USA. Indeed, one of the key players in the *Intrepid* empire, producer-writer-actor Nick Cook, has travelled to America to appear in other amateur *Trek* movies there. Along with his fellow multi-tasking team-member Steve Hammond (director-writer-camera operator-editor-special effects), Cook is looking to branch out beyond the deck of the *Intrepid* and move into making original science fiction and other genre films.

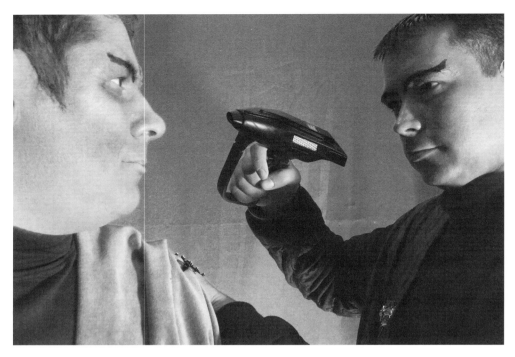

On the set of the *Starship Intrepid*: Romulan guard David Robertson points a phaser at David Reid, playing Vulcan Lieutenant S'Ceris. *(Nick Cook)*

Klingon Chief D'Gor (Alain DeMol) and Lieutenant S'Ceris (David Reid) shelter from the Dundee rain on a shoot for *Starship Intrepid*. *(Nick Cook)*

three

BIG CATS

If by some miracle of time travel a Victorian researcher into the paranormal could see a book published on the subject in the twenty-first century, he (let's assume it's a he) would find much of the subject matter very familiar. Just like their nineteenth-century forebears, modern researchers are still writing about ghosts, precognitive visions and dreams, witchcraft, magic, psychic powers, and encounters with fairies and other other-worldly beings. Two subjects, however, would cause the Victorian gentleman to scratch his head in perplexity: UFOs and big cats. Although strange things have been reported in the sky from the Middle Ages and earlier, it's only since 1947 that flying saucers or extraterrestrial spacecraft have been part of our consciousness. And the 'big cat' phenomenon is even more recent, not becoming fully established until the 1970s.

What are 'alien big cats'?

The basic idea is that big cats that normally live in Africa, Asia or the Americas have found a niche in the British countryside. Because of their overseas origin the creatures are often called 'exotic non-native species' or 'alien big cats' (shortened to ABCs). Hundreds of sightings have been logged around the UK, dozens of them in the Dundee area. The most common descriptions are of two kinds: a tawny-coloured animal resembling a puma (known as a cougar or mountain lion in the USA), or the smaller, tufted-eared lynx; and a black cat with the appearance of a black panther (a melanistic version of the leopard). How is it possible that such exotic feline predators could be roaming Britain? The possible answers come in several categories:

1. *The animals are former pets.* Until 1976 anyone could own a big cat without a licence. Although many such creatures were no doubt cared for by genuine animal lovers, others were owned by the kind of people who enjoyed the dubious status of owning a fearsome big cat, irrespective of the animal's welfare. Then the Dangerous Wild Animals Act was passed, requiring all large predators to be licensed and kept in enclosures of a minimum size. Many owners, not wanting to have their animals put down or rehoused – or not willing to pay the additional costs for the licence and secure pens – irresponsibly released their cats into the wild. Other cats simply escaped. There is a great deal of evidence for this; for example, the Big Cats in Scotland organisation (BCIS) has heard from a Dundee woman who rescued a cat in the 1970s. Only when it grew bigger did she realise it was a leopard. After it became obvious the creature was

too dangerous to keep at home, it was rehoused at a farm. But predators are true to their nature, and after the leopard moved from rats, rabbits and pheasants to the farmer's lambs, the shotgun came out. The startled leopard took to the Sidlaw Hills. Leopards can live for a maximum of twenty years, so this creature must now be dead; but if it managed to find a mate, its offspring could still be in the area.

2. *The animals are 'spirit creatures'.* This view, that ABCs move between our world and some kind of other reality, is prompted by their apparent ghost-like quality. Typically, there are a series of sightings by the public in the area, but when police forces and dog trackers are mobilised, no evidence is found of a cat – no tracks, no spoor, no remains of carcasses. Melanistic black panthers are also very rare in the wild, yet they form the majority of descriptions from sightings, which suggests something else might be afoot. Further, some black cats have been seen in places where black 'fairy dogs' or 'hounds of hell' have been reported for centuries, leading some to think that sightings of black cats are modern versions of these folkloric 'Black Dogs' (also known as Black Shuck, Cu Sith, Barguest and Padfoot, the latter name familiar to fans of Harry Potter's shapeshifting uncle Sirius Black).

Against the supernatural explanation is some incontrovertible physical evidence: a live puma was found in Inverness-shire (its stuffed body is in Inverness Museum); bodies of smaller exotic creatures such as jungle cats have been seen and photographed in the Scottish Borders; and a puma skull has been exhumed in Devon. Further, we are dealing with some of the most cunning and patient predators on the planet. In their natural habitat big cats, especially leopards, are expert at remaining invisible even when enemies such as baboons are active just a few feet away, and can remain perfectly still for many hours at a time. Leopards can pad through African villages or even shanty towns without being seen, while even experienced hunters in North America can miss a cougar (puma) as it lies hidden nearby. Some of the evidence presented in the following cases also seems to contradict the otherwordly hypothesis.

3. *The sightings are cases of mistaken identity.* In this view, people are genuinely seeing flesh-and-blood animals, but they are incorrect in identifying them as pumas or panthers. Candidates for the real animals include: the rare Scottish Wildcat; hybrids between the Wildcat and domestic cats, which tend to be larger and more aggressive than ordinary moggies; descendants of domestic cats that have gone feral; and unusual breeds or examples of domestic cats. A good example of the latter – and a case study in why eyewitnesses are not always reliable – took place near Ninewells Hospital on 3 August 2007. As reported in the *Courier* the following day, a couple out walking their dog behind the houses off the access road to the accident and emergency department saw a cat with a glossy coat, yellow eyes and sharp pointed ears. It was bigger than the couple's cocker spaniel, which would not approach the animal. They were adamant the strange creature was not a domestic cat, and thought it was

a lynx. Two days later a bemused cat-owner contacted the paper, which printed a photograph of the culprit – Callum, a glossy-coated, yellow-eyed and pointed-eared pedigree Maine Coon domestic cat. Callum was certainly bigger than a cocker spaniel – he was 3ft long from his nose to the tip of his tail, and weighed nearly 21lbs (10kg) – but was described as shy, gentle and docile. Not a lynx, then.

The first big cat spotted in the general Dundee/Angus area seems to have been in February 1979, when a 'large, black, cat-like creature' was seen twice on the same day in the snow-covered fields around Kilry, between Alyth and Glen Isla. The report in the *Sunday Post* said the animal was 'bigger than any domestic cat or dog' and about 2ft high. It is possible this was the leopard that escaped a few years earlier, (see category 1).

Big cats in the 1990s

Things then seem to have been quiet – or at least there were no *reported* sightings – until the early summer of 1994, when a large black cat was seen by multiple witnesses at Crombie Country Park, Ninewells Hospital, Ledcrief Fisheries near Tullybaccart in Perthshire, and Old Downie Farm, north of Newbigging near Monifieth – all of which is a mighty territory for one animal to cover in a short time (although cats in the wild can have territories 30 miles across). There were more sightings at Whigstreet, five miles south of Forfar, at Linlathen Nursing Home near Balgillo in Broughty Ferry, and in the Muirdrum area. A black cat was also spotted in early August in Checkiefield, by Kirriemuir, while there were two sightings near Downie Den, Tannadice in November and again in January 1995.

The year 1995 started badly for Shirley Kerr, who lost two sheep to a mystery predator that stripped the carcasses on her farm north of Monifieth. As she told the *Courier* on 4 January, the nature of the butchery was not characteristic of humans or dogs, and furthermore, one of the victims was a large Jacob ewe with frightening horns: 'Even our own sheepdogs were nervous of this ewe, it was so big.' On 3 March the 'Angus cat' – or one of them – moved closer to urban locations, when it was flushed out of some undergrowth by a dog being walked on the path near the Esplanade in Broughty Ferry. Frank Donnelly and Elma Lowson described the animal as black and puma-like, and taller and longer than their adult border collie, with a rounded head and long tail (note that pumas are tawny-coloured, not black). A similar animal, 'a big black cat, the size of a labrador,' was spotted by John Tervit as he walked his dogs one morning in late March on the grassy area between Myrekirk Road roundabout and the traffic-choked Kingsway, while a woman saw a black puma-like creature running alongside a road in the west end of Dundee. Another cat was reported in the same month crossing the Forfar to Montrose road.

May 1995 was another busy month. Lee Mason saw a large, very fast black cat cross his path in a park between East Craigie and Gotterstone, again in a built-up area. On the 11th a 'collie-sized' black cat with a small head and long tail was seen at Crombie Park and warnings were posted in the park. In contrast to the usual 'black cat' sightings, a brown rust-coloured animal was spotted by Audrey Bain and Garry McDonald on the Auchterhouse-Tealing road: 'It's face was the same shape as a Doberman's with really wee, pointy ears, but it definitely had a slim, cat-like body,' Audrey told the *Courier*. 'I've never seen anything like it in my life. It looked really evil – there's no way I'd go anywhere near it.' A second sighting of a beige-coloured animal took place in Dundee on the 29th. And in September 2009 a former taxi driver, now resident in the USA, posted a 1995 sighting on the website of the *Arbroath Herald*: 'I was heading to Condor with a fare on the Forfar Road near Rosely Country House and it would have been between 11 p.m. and 1 a.m. The animal…was light brown in colour and the size of a Great Dane but the tail was much longer and appeared to have a black end on it and a heavier body.'

On 18 January 1996 a motorist saw a big cat in his headlights on the Esplanade in Broughty Ferry. The animal bolted and disappeared into the undergrowth by the railway line on the Monifieth side of Buddies nightclub – exactly the same place as witnessed by Frank Donnelly and Elma Lowson some nine months previously. 'It was the size of a big dog, but more of a cat's body,' the driver told the *Evening Telegraph* the following day. 'It had a huge grey tail that trailed along the ground. The tail was bushy and the animal appeared furry with pointed ears.' Sometime in 1996 there was also a sighting in Strathmartine Road, in the grounds of Strathmartine Hospital. The cats (or cats) seemed to go to ground for a number of months after this, the next being reported on December 1997 when on two occasions the water bailiff of Rescobie Loch near Forfar saw a 'bright-eyed, large cat-like animal', and a few days later a black cat 'bigger than a large dog' was seen bounding across the A92 near the Panbride turn-off to Carnoustie. The following week pest control officers visited the derelict Beatties Bakery on Clepington Road after a report of a large, black, cat-like animal there. According to the *Evening Telegraph* on 18 December, 'massive claw markings' were found on a mud bank at the nearby St Francis football ground.

In 1998 the cat went golfing. On 21 April Bill Duncan, the greenkeeper at the golf course near Cotside Farm, Barry, saw a large black cat chasing sheep in the adjacent fields; the following

The Esplanade at Broughty Ferry. Several big cats have been sighted near here. *(Geoff Holder)*

day a lamb was found savaged, and Mr Duncan told the *Courier* on the 24th that several workers and golfers had seen the animal previously. Then, on 15 October, Alistair Malcolm, the greenkeeper of Buddon Links, Carnoustie, saw a large black cat running across the fairway and into nearby woodland. It was 'bigger than a Labrador' with a long tail and a short nose. A dead swan with its head missing was also found. And in December a sheep's leg was discovered near the starters' box at the Ashludie Links in Monifieth – the first of several possible big cat-related incidents on the golf course. In January 2009 a contributor to the *Scotsman* website recorded a sighting in a field near Lundie from June 1999. It was 'a large, black, puma-like cat around three feet long' and had just previously been seen by two anglers at a fishery.

Post-millennium cats

On 27 January 2000 farmer Graham Anderson from Abernyte saw *two* puma-like animals chasing his sheep. 'I saw two cats bounding over the dyke in one of my fields,' he told the *Courier*. 'They stopped when they saw me and whenever I moved they just took off. I've lived in the area most of my life and I know a wild cat when I see one. These things were four or maybe six times the size of a wild cat. There's no doubt in my mind what I saw were pumas.' In October 2000 it was Carnoustie's turn again, with multiple sightings, including an animal 'a lot bigger than a dog' seen from a house on Burnside Gardens. Laura Colliston and Maureen Strachan guessed the 'light brown to ginger' creature was a lynx. A motorist on the road to Scryne picked out a pair of glowing eyes in his headlights, followed by a sighting of a cat-like animal with a curved tail. An almost exactly identical sighting was made by a driver on the road linking East Haven with the A92 – eyes shining in the dark, followed by a view of a lynx-like cat about the size of a dog, 'a mix of tan and black in colour'. Another sighting of a cat with glowing eyes bounding across the A92 dual carriageway – this time at Inverkeilor, on the way to Montrose – was reported on 3 January 2001.

The next crop of sightings was in the summer of 2001. On 18 July a rush-hour motorist saw a jet-black cat with a long slim body and large piercing eyes by Ashludie Hospital, on the outskirts of Monifieth. 'It was running gracefully through the undergrowth, arching its back while it ran. All of a sudden it changed direction and disappeared into the trees,' Ian Clark told the *Evening Telegraph*. 'I half thought about stopping to take a closer look, but I quickly decided against it, as seeing it from the car was frightening enough, let alone coming face-to-face with it.' On 24 August what was possibly the same black panther-type animal was spotted in a field opposite the houses at Fairway, close to the B962, the road from east Monifieth to the A92. Later in the year there were two sightings within a week, further north at Inverbervie and Edzell, and at the end of March 2002 the Ashludie area was the site of another encounter when a Monifieth resident briefly saw 'a black panther about four foot in length' near the golf course.

Two detailed sightings

An unusually detailed account of a sighting was given by Carolann Curran to the *Courier* on 4 June 2002. The Monikie student had been driving towards Dundee late on the previous Sunday night: 'I was coming down past the new houses at Ballumbie and travelling slowly as I came round a bend,' she said, continuing:

I'm not good with feet or metres but I would say I was the distance between two lamp posts away when I saw it and slowed right down. It was 11.06 p.m., I looked at the clock in the car. The first thing I noticed was the size of it and the size of its tail. I am not saying it was an enormous thing like a panther or a tiger. I have a Staffordshire bull terrier and I would say the body was about the same height. It looked really fit and the way it got up on the dyke at the side of the road was very athletic. It wasn't like it went to jump on the dyke to get out of the way of the car, it was more like it didn't want to walk through the wet grass and it just got down on its haunches and was up on the dyke. That was when I noticed the length of its tail, coming down in a curve and stretching out behind its body. It seemed completely intent on what it was doing and didn't even look round at the car as I drove very slowly past it.

On 5 June there was a similar sighting in the same paper, a Monikie man reporting a big black cat with 'a blunt face' on the B961 near the village. The animal's most striking feature was its 'long thick tail'.

A second well-observed description appeared in the *Courier* on 23 September. The previous Saturday (the 21st) an off-duty police officer watched an 'unmistakably feline' animal for twenty minutes as it prowled around a newly-harvested cereal field on the outskirts of Carnoustie, near the main East Coast rail line. 'In the course of my work and leisure activities, I reckon I have seen just about every wild and domesticated animal there should be in Scotland,' the officer said:

This, however, was something I have never seen before. I'm now wholly convinced there are animals living around us that are not part of the natural fauna. I was 150-200 yards from the cat and watched it for a good while through binoculars. Although it was jet-black, the only animal I would liken it to in general size and build is a lynx. Having walked across the field after the animal disappeared I was able to gauge its size against the tussocks of grass and the fence. I would estimate it to have stood a good two feet at the shoulder and easily four feet in length. This was not a large domestic cat, a dog or a fox ... It was definitely a cat of a type I have never come across before.

The same month, George Mackie passed on a sighting made by the wife of one of his friends of a cat on a rise near the dumping ground by Shanwell Cemetery in Carnoustie, and on 10 October Ian and Shelagh Paterson were driving along the A92 between Arbroath and Dundee when they spotted 'a large black cat, well over a metre in length from head to tail and about the size of a full-grown puma.' On 28 October there was a second sighting in the area, this time at Hatton, near Arbroath.

A David Attenborough moment

A much more urban location was the setting for an encounter late at night on 21 September. A couple were driving east along Drumgeith Road between Whitfield and Baldovie when a large animal shot across the road. 'I reckon it went from one side of the main road to the other in no more than three bounds before disappearing into the bushes and undergrowth,' the anonymous man told the *Evening Telegraph* on 24 September. 'This animal was at least the size of a very large dog and was jet black and it had a thick, round tail like a cat rather than a bushy tail like a fox …This thing looked for all the world like a big cat – the sort of thing you'd expect to see on a David Attenborough wildlife programme rather than crossing the road in Dundee on a Friday night.'

A Wildcat?

A very unusual sighting took place in Broughty Ferry in 2003. From his front window Walter Crerar of Dunalistair Gardens saw what he was convinced was a Scottish Wildcat. 'All my life I have gone hillwalking and have always known what a wildcat looks like but I have never seen anything like this,' he was quoted as saying in the *Courier* on 28 February.

> The cat was around four feet long, like a little panther, was light grey and had a distinctive ringed tail which was grey and white. The big cat was facing up to a moggy that lives in the street and was gradually creeping towards it before it got distracted and both cats dashed away. I called some friends who live in the country and who I know have seen wildcats themselves and they said my description matches what they have seen perfectly.

Wildcats, a native species, usually live in remote parts of the Highlands.

Critters and cubs

More sightings took place in urban areas in September 2005, when a large black cat was spotted near the BP garage on the Kingsway, and a few weeks later three people in a car on Riverside Drive at 2.30 in the morning saw a similar animal dash across the road at great speed. The following month Russell Girling of Newhall Gardens in the west end found a cat 'at least the size of a Labrador' in his garden at night – when disturbed the animal speedily leapt over the back wall. Later in the year Monifieth was back in the big cat sightings league – on the morning of 23 October, former provost and chairman of Monifieth Town Council Ian Mortimer witnessed a 'well-fed' animal 'about the size of a collie dog' jump over a fence beside the football pitches next to the caravan park by the beach, while, in one of the most astonishing encounters, May Mulholland was in her living room on Panmure Street when she saw a puma *and its cub* curled up in the tree opposite. The greyish-brown adult had a long, thin tail and had wrapped itself around the trunk, with the cub – distinguished by its stripes – sitting on its back. The tree was in the grounds of St Mary's Hospital. 'I phoned across to St Mary's,' May told the *Courier* on 24 December, 'and they said they hadn't seen their squirrels for two or three days.'

Yet another brief encounter took place in February 2006 when both taxi driver Derek Neil and his fare saw a black puma-like animal swiftly cross the road in the grounds of Liff Hospital. There were more sightings in Dundee, Carnoustie and Monifieth in April, and in July two people saw a 'panther-like' creature at the back of Strathmartine Bowling Club in Rosemill. Out in the rural areas, cat were spotted in countryside near Brechin (February 2007), Forfar (March 2007) and Fowlis (December 2007), while on the last day of the year paw prints five and a half inches long were found in the bunker at the 14th fairway of Camperdown Golf Course. The year 2009 brought several reports of sightings from around the Kirkton area of Arbroath and the golf course at Letham Grange.

So what is going on?

As we saw with Callum the Maine Coon pedigree, some of these sightings may be cases of mistaken identity. But even if only a portion of the cases are accurate, there seems good evidence that there have been several big cats living in Angus. At least one is black, and another is rust-coloured. Of course, big cats do not live longer than twenty years, so perhaps the animals spotted in the 1990s are now dead. However two witnesses have seen two cats at the same time (one apparently a cub), which suggests there has been a breeding population (and hence at least four adult cats, two male and two female). The Carnoustie/Monifieth corridor seems one hotspot, while at least one cat has ventured into the suburbs and busy roads of the city of Dundee itself (this behaviour has also been reported of 'urban leopards' feeding on the fringes of the sprawling shanty towns around African cities). Although definitive proof is lacking, all in all Dundee's 'alien big cats' seem to be the phenomenon most likely to be proved genuine in the near future. Intriguingly, there have been no reports up to the time of writing (April 2010) – did the cats succumb to the exceptionally cold winter of 2009/10?

four

ALL CREATURES GREAT AND SMALL (AND WEIRD AND WONDERFUL)

In many ways Alien Big Cats are a classic example of 'out of place animals'. One of the less celebrated but utterly compelling aspects of paranormal research is hunting down examples of animals turning up where according to conventional wisdom they have no right to be, or creatures doing things that are unconventional or downright bizarre. There is a colony of wallabies on an island in Loch Lomond, several South American coatimundis can be found in the Lake District, while other parts of the UK boast 'winged' cats, legends of extinct Australian thylacines, and even something apparently called the Loch Ness Monster.

The first case here, however, is not just about the animal itself, but what was found *inside* it…

Inside the belly of the beast

The skeleton of the 'Famous Tay Whale' hangs in the McManus Galleries in Dundee, accompanied by the poem of the same name, written by William McGonagall. (Don't worry, I'm not going to quote any of McGonagall's infamously bad work here; but those who enjoy his cultural reputation may be interested to know that he has been folklorically immortalised in Terry Pratchett's *Discworld* novel *The Wee Free Men*. When the diminutive but dangerous pixies of the title cannot overcome an adversary by fighting, they wheel out their most dangerous weapon – their bard, whose title is simply 'mcgonagall'. A few lines of atrociously mangled verse spouted by a skilled mcgonagall will send the most vicious enemy scurrying for cover, hands over their ears.)

For years I believed the whale had become stranded on a sandbar in the Tay, and indeed that bowdlerised version of its history can still be found on a number of websites. The truth is rather less palatable. In December 1883 the whale – a humpback, a rare sighting off the coasts of Britain – entered the Tay, where it entertained vast crowds with the breaching displays so beloved of whale-watchers. Despite the fact that humpbacks contain so little oil as to be commercially negligible, some Dundee whalers set out to harpoon the animal that 'dared' to flaunt its presence within sight of the nation's premier whaling fleet; and soon the crowds that had been enraptured by the spectacle of the whale's antics, were now cheering on the whalers as they attempted to annihilate the graceful giant.

It did not go as the whalers planned – in fact, the hunt was conducted with equal amounts of inhumanity and ineptitude. Despite being grievously wounded by harpoons, metal bolts, hand-lances and other ironmongery, the 40ft-long beast still had the strength to drag two

The Bell Rock Lighthouse on Inchcape Rock, in the Firth of Tay. The whale dragged the boats beyond here. *(Perth & Kinross Libraries)*

six-oared rowing boats, a steam launch and an ironclad steam tug out of the estuary, past the Bell Rock lighthouse and into the open sea. Over the next twenty-two hours the severely hemorrhaging humpback pulled a dead weight of between 20 and 30 tons a distance of 50 miles, a truly awesome feat of endurance which merely serves to emphasize the wonder and majesty of these magnificent mammals. Finally the lines broke, the exhausted whalers gratefully headed back home and the whale swam off to an ignominious and painful death on the high seas.

Some time later the carcass was recovered and put on exhibition in Dundee by John Wood, an oil merchant, would-be show-business impresario and astute entrepreneur better known as 'Greasy Johnny'. Part of the 'show' involved the famous scientist Sir John Struthers, Professor of Anatomy at the University of Aberdeen, reluctantly dissecting the whale in front of a paying audience. As part of this process, over three tonnes of intestines, plus the stomach, was sent to Glasgow University for further analysis. And then came the surprise…

The Tay whale
Astounding Discovery!
A Man Found in the Stomach!
(By Extra Special Wire)

That was the headline in the Dundee *Advertiser* on 8 February 1884. The paper's reporter had sent off the amazing dispatch at 2 p.m. from Glasgow:

Extraordinary excitement prevails in Glasgow owing to the discovery this forenoon of a live man in the stomach of the Tay whale … A number of the University Professors and other scientific gentlemen were present by invitation, as also several clergymen and prominent citizens. About noon a large incision was made, and the stomach partially opened, when something in the nature of a solid obstruction was encountered.

The nature of the 'solid obstruction' soon became evident:

> Curiosity changed into utter amazement when, on the incision being enlarged and the upper portions of the stomach being carefully drawn back, the obstruction was found to be a human being, lying in an easy position, as in sleep, with the body bent; with the right arm, which was underneath, doubled at the elbow; and the side of the nose resting on the forefinger.

It was supposed at first that the man was dead, but on examination he was found to be breathing. Shouting in his ear produced no response, so electrical resuscitation was attempted: 'Two powerful batteries of sixteen horse power have been applied, but without producing the slightest effect.' Meanwhile things became, amazingly, even more bizarre. The Revd John Smith, one of the clergymen invited to the dissection, seemed to have an onrush of religious idiocy, declaring that 'the man was no other than the prophet Jonah, and that the whale and the unfaithful prophet had both been preserved miraculously, and been directed to these shores as a triumphant refutation of modern scepticism.' Some in the crowd disputed this, pointing out that in the Biblical story the whale was said to have vomited Jonah up, so this man could not be Jonah and this could not be Jonah's whale. The good reverend countered this by cunningly claiming that the whale, at the direction of God, had swallowed Jonah again.

Sadly for John Smith's Old Testament fantasies, one of the observers present, William Sanderson of Newport-on-Tay, recognised the stomach-dweller as a tramp well-known in the Dundee area as 'the Autocrat of the Tay Ferries'. So adamant was Sanderson about this identification that he said he was prepared 'to take affidavit that this was the man' (it sounds like Mr Sanderson was irritated by the Revd Smith's enthusiasms for survivals from the Bible).

Also found in the whale's stomach were scores of dead herring and sprats, the smoke-blackened glass funnel of an oil lamp of the same make as used on the Tay Ferry steamers, and a large pocket-book. If this had been an adventure novel, the pocket-book would have contained the last words of the voyager, revealing how he came to be swallowed by a whale, but it turned out to be rather disappointing:

> It was found to contain a large number of musty papers which did not appear to have been touched in a long time. As the first scrap of paper was being opened, the Rev. Mr Smith, who adhered firmly to his conviction that the man was Jonah, expressed his opinion from the faded appearance of the paper that it would prove to be a Tarshish or Nineveh bank-note [both Tarshish and Nineveh were nations mentioned in the Old Testament]. On closer examination, however, it was found to be an account for 'ten gallons of inferior oil for saloon'.

This was accompanied by some rather dull printed mottos and pieces of long out-of-date correspondence that seemed to have been penned by someone connected with the ferries. It was not clear whether the book had belonged to the tramp; more likely he had stolen it or it had arrived in the leviathan's stomach fortuitously.

Meanwhile, the scientists present had been poring over the unconscious man. His pulse and breathing were very slow. Phrenology, the pseudo-science where savants claimed to be able to determine personality by examining the 'lumps and bumps' of the head, was all the rage at the time, so the doctors didn't miss this opportunity: 'the bump of Aggravativeness covers the entire area usually occupied by the moral faculties.' In other words, this man's skull-shape supposedly revealed that he was very violent and lacked any conscience. There was still a slight hope of reviving him: 'Guns are to be fired this afternoon close to the exposed ear; but the doctors doubt if they will produce any movement or response.'

So, having passed through Biblical fantasies, phrenology, resuscitation by electricity and gunshot, there is still the central mystery: how did the man get into the belly of the whale? The stomach was removed in the dissecting yard in Dundee on 25 January, put in a sealed barrel, sent to Aberdeen and then reshipped to Glasgow, so by 8 February he must have been there at least two weeks. There seem to be three possibilities:

1. He fell off the ferry as the whale was disporting in the Firth of Tay, and was swallowed as the humpback was hoovering up the herrings that had attracted it to the river mouth in the first place.

2. Possibly befuddled by drink, the tramp had been seeking somewhere warm to sleep and crawled into the stomach when it was still within Greasy Johnny's yard in Dundee before the dissection. Theoretically this was possible, as thousands of people came to see the whale during this time, and the mouth was kept propped open so that people could have their photo taken in 'the jaws of the beast'.

3. It was all a hoax. This is the possibility considered by Jim Crumley, who first brought this story to public attention in *The Winter Whale*, his superb book on the whole sorry saga of the Tay Whale. The report in the *Advertiser* was the only mention in the press. Perhaps the editor realised he had been duped by the reporter, and the lack of follow-up in print reflected the paper's embarrassment.

In *The Winter Whale* Crumley also points out, by the way, that the 'Famous Tay Whale' was a late juvenile or young adult, and humpbacks can live for a very, very long time; if it had not been pointlessly slaughtered it might still be alive today, singing its oceanic songs to the many descendents it never had a chance to sire. It's something to think about when viewing the titanic skeleton in the McManus Galleries.

Whale meat again

The Tay Whale was only the second recorded humpback to perish on British shores, the first being cast ashore about two miles north of Berwick-upon-Tweed on 19 September 1829, with six cormorants in its stomach and a seventh stuck in its throat – this last meal may have been what choked it. Back in the Tay estuary, meanwhile, it seems other whales were rare, but not unknown. According to A.C. Lamb's *Dundee: Its Quaint and Historic Buildings*, fourteen 'Finners' were captured on the shore at Mylnefield, near Invergowrie, in October 1808, the largest being 23ft long. In October 1817 nearly forty Finners appeared in the river and were chased onto the shore and killed. And in August 1820 an enormous specimen, $50\frac{1}{2}$ft long and 25ft in circumference, was captured at the mouth of the Tay. All these episodes took place before Dundee became a major whaling port. The 'Famous Tay Whale' was unusual in that it was a humpback and stayed in the Firth for several weeks, and unfortunate in that it arrived when dozens of whaling men were sitting around during the winter lay-off.

The Tay Sea Serpent

The Tay has also seen large marine visitors in more recent times. In September 1932, for instance, the *Courier* noted that a whale 'over 40 feet in length' had been spotted near the Bell Rock. But nothing compares to the same paper's report of 28 July 1958 – a sighting of an honest-to-goodness sea serpent. The principal witness was bus driver Ronald Avery, who described what had happened the previous Saturday (the 26th):

> The bus was standing at the Newport-on-Tay terminus. We were waiting for the starting time and I was standing on the step of the bus looking over the water. It was misty, but about five minutes to eight I saw distinctly, about a mile out from Newport Pier, a strange creature moving in the water. Three humps were visible and although it was difficult to tell their colouring I thought they were dark. They were moving towards the Tay Bridge. They disappeared, and then came to the surface again in exactly the same manner a short distance forward.

Mr Avery pointed out the creature to the conductress Betty Kay and together they watched as it swam towards the rail bridge. 'We must have seen it disappear and surface eight or nine times,' he said, continuing:

Newport-on-Tay in the early twentieth century. From this general area a sea serpent was sighted in 1958.
(Perth & Kinross Libraries)

It made a circle towards some boats near the opposite bank. Then it was time for us to move, but I was so impressed that I reported it to the police. I would say it was a sea snake or serpent, about 15 to 20 feet in length. I don't think the object I saw was porpoises or seals. I've seen sharks and whales in the Indian Ocean but this was the strangest thing I have ever seen in the water.

As far as I can tell there was no follow up to this extraordinary event, and no further sightings were reported.

God is in the Bible; the Bible is in the cod

The following story appeared in the *Irish Times* on 7 March 1874, concerning a codfish caught by a Dundee fisherman:

On being opened for cleaning purposes it was discovered, greatly to the astonishment of the cook, that this wonderful and pious fish contained in that domestic department, commonly called the stomach, a Bible bound in calf, bearing on the title-page the name of William Sim, and the date 1830. A cod's stomach is exceedingly powerful, but the digestion of a Bible bound in calf was beyond the capacity of this intelligent fish.

Hook, line and cannibal

In August 1930 the *Courier* told how Dundee angler Walter Morrison had, with one hook, caught two trout simultaneously, one inside the other. His prize was landed in the River Isla – the hook was in the smaller fish, which had been swallowed entire by the larger trout.

Toad in the hole

There is a theme that regularly crops up in the annals of paranormal research – the 'entombed toad', which tells of a toad found alive inside a rock, where no animal could survive. One such episode comes from Dundee. In 1830 the witness, who signed himself 'Geographer' in a letter to a Glasgow paper two years later, visited a whinstone quarry 'two miles east of Dundee' (this might be Ardownie Quarry). There he watched as a quarryman struck a large grey boulder near the entrance: 'At the third well directed blow the one half of the boulder fell away, relieving, at the same time, a live toad of the largest size usually seen in this country.' The worker was accompanied by his young son, who had brought his lunch; as the toad crawled away, the boy killed it. 'Geographer' then went on to describe the space occupied by the animal. 'It was in size and shape like a goose egg, inside the cavity smooth as the polished marble, and surrounding it the grey whin was discoloured to ⅜ths of an inch to a dark brown.'

Dozens of similar examples are recorded in the nineteenth century and some researchers think it is simply a 'tall tale' that did the rounds of newspapers and magazines as a 'silly season' story. On the other hand, some of the detailed material collected on the subject around the world has led some scientists to suggest toads can survive in confined places for several years; so the 'Dundee toad' may have been real, and even if it may not have been in the rock for millennia, it is still an indication of how weird nature can be.

Here be dragons

I was tempit at Pitempton,
Draiglet at Baldragon,
Stricken at Strikemartin,
And killed at Martinstane.

The 'I' in this traditional rhyme is Dundee's last (and only) dragon. The story goes that a farmer lived at Pitempton, north of Downfield, with his nine beautiful daughters, their virtues described in another old ballad:

Nine maidens were they spotless fair,
With silver skins, bright golden hair,
Blue-eyed, vermilion-cheeked, nowhere
Their match in Glen of Ogilvy.

(Silver skins? What were they, aliens?) Anyway, one evening the eldest girl went to the well for water but did not return. The second daughter went searching for her, but also vanished. Soon the third, fourth, fifth, sixth, seventh, eighth and finally the ninth girls were missing, leading the father to suspect something was up. The tale is taken up in typical Victorian style by Robert Chambers in his book *Popular Rhymes of Scotland*:

He then seized his fish-spear and ran to the well, where he discovered a monstrous serpent, or dragon, lying besmeared with blood, apparently having killed and devoured all the nine unfortunate maidens. Unable to cope single-handed with so formidable a foe, the poor man retreated in dismay; but having quickly collected several hundreds of his neighbours, he soon returned to the place, and prepared to attack the monster, which had thus deprived him of all earthly comfort.

The Nine Maidens pub on Laird Street, named for the victims of the Pitempton Dragon. (*Geoff Holder*)

What then took place was a kind of running battle between the retreating dragon and the attacking peasants (no doubt the proceedings also involved pitchforks and flaming torches). The reptile first moved a few hundred yards northwest to a place now called Baldragon, which was then a marsh, hence the creature being 'Draiglit ('wetted') at Baldragon'. Still harassed, the creature fled a couple of miles north, where it was attacked by a young man named Martin, the sweetheart of one of the slaughtered maidens. Empowered by the rage of revenge, Martin smote the dragon a great blow with his club. Thinking the dragon defeated, he turned his back on his scaly foe, but the monster still had life, and was about to devour the lad when the villagers cried in warning, 'Strike, Martin!' Martin immediately whirled round and smacked the dragon a second time. For this reason the place was known as Strikemartin (now corrupted to Strathmartine).

The grievously wounded dragon now crawled a short distance north, where it was surrounded by the peasants (pitchforks at the ready) and finally despatched by the heroic Martin. To demonstrate the truth of all this, a stone, known as Martin's Stone, still stands on the spot, and is sculptured with the outlined figure of a serpent.

Martin's Stone is actually a Pictish cross-slab dating from AD 700-850. The top of the stone – the part carved with the cross itself – has been broken off, and all that remains are the enigmatic Pictish figures whose exact meaning still inspires scholarly controversy. Sadly the surviving carvings are difficult to make out. There is a fragment of a mounted rider, then below that another horseman, the strange 'Pictish beast' (known variously as the 'swimming elephant' or the 'dolphin') and a snake sinuously entwined around a 'Z-rod' symbol. It stands, surrounded by a metal railing, in the middle of a field southwest of South Balluderon on the minor road between Strathmartine and Balgray. If the field is in crop there is no access. Several more Pictish carved stones have been found at Strathmartine, one of which has two serpents biting each other. This stone, which used to stand opposite the west gate of the churchyard, is now in the McManus Galleries. It is possible that these mysterious carved stones may have given rise to the story of the dragon fight and slaying.

From the descriptions in the traditional story, it is clear the dragon is not winged (otherwise it would fly away). It therefore seems to be a *worm* (also spelled *worme* or *wurm*), a huge serpent-like reptile with a massive head filled with ferocious teeth, but lacking wings or limbs. Worms are the most common dragons found in Scotland and Scandinavia. The Strathmartine dragon has prompted some local artworks, most famously the wonderful metal dragon, sculpted by Tony Morrow, that adorns Murraygate, just a few yards from the site of the former Beldragon House. Sidlaw View Primary School, a little east of Baldragon Academy on Harestane Road, has a sculpture of a sinuous *worm* in its grounds, created by local artist Steve Thomson in 2007.

Meanwhile St Andrew's Church on the Cowgate, the second oldest standing church in Dundee, built in 1774, has for its weathervane a species of winged, two-legged dragon known as a wyvern (the parish magazine is also called *The Wyvern*). Wyverns were traditionally guardians of treasure, which seems appropriate as St Andrew's was once called the Trades' Kirk, being founded by the men of trade and commerce of the Nine Trades of Dundee. Along with part of the steeple, the wyvern came crashing down on 9 September 1970 when lightning hit the church at 10.30 a.m. Four people in a doorway 100 yards away were blasted back several

The dragon coiled around a lamppost on Murraygate. (*Geoff Holder*)

Above: The splendid dragon in the garden of Sidlaw View Primary School. (*Ségolène Dupuy*)

Left: Baldragon Academy, a short distance from the Sidlaw View dragon. (*Geoff Holder*)

The wyvern that protects St Andrew's Church on Cowgate. *(Geoff Holder)*

feet and landed on a flight of steps leading into a shop. Victim George Minto said, 'The flash of lightning was absolutely blinding. There was a tremendous report as the steeple was struck and we all closed our eyes. The next thing we knew we were lying on the steps.' A radiogram playing inside Watt's store on Wellgate blew up as the lightning lit up the sky, and three men unloading television sets took shelter seconds before the rubble threw their van 15ft across the pend and split it in two. The *Courier* estimated 2.25 million tons of rain had poured down in just ninety minutes, which translated into an astonishing rainfall of 1.86 inches. The steeple was repaired and the replacement wyvern still tilts with the wind.

The incredible journey

In the 1870s a Scottish gentleman working in Calcutta felt the need for a companion from his homeland, so he wrote to a friend near Inverkeithing requesting he send 'a good Scotch collie dog'. The dog duly arrived in India, but then unaccountably disappeared. A few weeks later, to the astonishment of the Inverkeithing man, the collie turned up at his house. The animal was healthy and well-fed, but how he had travelled unaccompanied from India to Inverkeithing was a complete mystery, so enquiries were made. At Inverkeithing it was learned the dog had disembarked from a collier that had returned from Dundee. At Dundee, it was found that the intrepid animal had arrived on board a ship from Calcutta. There was no evidence from Calcutta, so Revd J.G. Wood, who published the case in his 1875 book *Man and Beast Here and Hereafter*, assumed that the homesick collie had recognised a Scottish accent among the men at the docks, and hidden away on the sailor's ship in the hope that at least it would end up somewhere familiar (another possibility is that the collie's finely-tuned olfactory sense picked up the scent of Scotland from one particular ship). How the dog identified an Inverkeithing-bound ship at Dundee was similarly puzzling, although perhaps it had previously seen (or smelt) the collier when it was in port at Inverkeithing. Whatever the explanation, it is still a remarkable example of the near-supernatural ability dogs have to return to familiar places (and faces), even if they are several thousand miles and two oceans away.

A similar if smaller-scale case was reported in the *Dundee Advertiser* on 2 June 1873. A Dundee man was so annoyed that his terrier, Beauty, kept running away to stay with a neighbour that he eventually moved to Aberdeen, taking the dog with him. Two months later Beauty turned up at the house of her preferred human in Dundee. She was emaciated and filthy, and had presumably walked the sixty or so miles between the two cities, despite having been taken to Aberdeen by train and being unfamiliar with the countryside of Angus and Kincardineshire.

In the *Courier* for 3 August 1827 there was the tale of a grocer in the Overgate who sold a Blairgowrie farmer a two-month-old puppy. The dog was carried to its new home in a sack, so was unable to see the surrounding countryside – but as soon as it was released at its new home, it promptly set off back to Dundee, covering the twenty-one miles from Blairgowrie in twelve hours. And in September 1928 the same paper covered the story of a five-year-old Airedale bitch named Peggie, who was temporarily left in Dundee while her owner returned to his home in Edinburgh. Peggie was deposited on Sunday evening, but early on Monday morning was found whining outside her door in Edinburgh, having apparently travelled over sixty miles, including presumably crossing the Firth of Forth by ferry, and enduring a severe thunderstorm. Not surprisingly, the devoted dog's paws were badly bruised.

Clever cats

Of course it's not just dogs who have homing instincts to make us marvel. On 17 June 1857 the *Courier* told the story of a cat sent from a house in Broughty Ferry to its new owner in the west end of Dundee. The animal, which had never left Broughty Ferry before, was popped into a covered basket and taken by a servant on the train to Dundee, the last part of the journey being completed by carriage. Having deposited the animal with its new human caretaker (cats don't really have *owners* as such), the servant made the return journey to Broughty Ferry. When he arrived back at his master's house, he found the cat at the door scratching to get in, the animal having covered the distance – perhaps five or six miles – faster than public transport. The same paper recorded a similar if opposite-directioned tale on 30 May 1873. A cat was taken in a covered basket by train from Dundee to its new home in Broughty Ferry. After two days it ran away, turning up exhausted at its former home eleven weeks later.

Cats can be remarkable in other ways, being both astonishingly stoic and sensitive. A newspaper report from 13 December 1842 stated that when a coal ship from Newcastle was being unloaded at Dundee, a cat was discovered in a tiny space among the coal. It was calculated that the animal must have been in the void – which was too small for it even to turn round – for at least fifteen days, without food or water. When rescued 'it appeared somewhat stupid' but soon recovered and was seen frisking about on deck. Another cat was trapped under the floorboards of a new building in a Dundee suburb for thirteen days, only being rescued when the new tenant heard its piteous cries. The story was in the *Courier* in May 1903. In August 1929 the same paper described how a black cat jumped off a third floor balcony and landed unhurt on Reform Street, 40ft below. 'Contrary to popular supposition,' said the report, 'it landed, not on its feet, but on its side. There were no bones broken, however, and after a dazed moment pussy scurried across the street and disappeared up a close.'

On 3 October 1851 the *Advertiser* told of a 20-year-old cat named Donald who had been the constant companion of a young, bed-ridden invalid for eight years. When his master eventually succumbed to the fatal illness, Donald was visibly grieving, and a short time later died himself. There was nature-defying fecundity when a cat in a flat off High Street had a litter of three kittens, then a second litter of two kittens only six days later, all the catkins being born hale and whole, while elsewhere a healthy litter of six contained four kittens born with their eyes open and working – most kittens open their eyes up to nine days after birth. The stories appeared in the *Advertiser* on 15 July 1842 and 24 July 1840 respectively.

Freaks of nature

Less edifying but nonetheless ghoulishly fascinating are examples of teratology, or genetic freaks, something nineteenth-century Dundee newspapers seemed obsessed with. A typical example is the case of a shipmaster's wife who found four newborn kittens sharing a common rear end. Each animal had its own tail, head and forefeet, but there was only one set of hips and rear legs between them – 'the hinder parts were one mass,' according to the report in the *Advertiser* on 6 September 1827. It mewed when picked up, but it was not clear if the sound came from just one throat or all four. The disgusted woman threw the *lusus naturae* ('whim of nature') over the harbour wall and into the water, where several men searched for it in the hope of selling it to a collector or naturalist, but the four-headed cat was not found.

Further freaks were recorded in the pages of the *Advertiser* over the following years. On 7 May 1841 a fish dealer in Crichton Street had a pair of 'Siamese kittens' joined at the belly, the combination having eight legs, four eyes, two tails and two noses, but only one mouth. It lived for about a month and after death was preserved in spirits. On 4 July 1844 it was reported that a cat owned by shop porter Robert Duff, who lived off Perth Road, had given birth to a litter of five kittens, one of which had two bodies joined near the neck channelling into a single head. One of the conjoined kittens was male, the other female; the combination died shortly after birth, but happily all the other new arrivals were healthy. On 28 September 1849 a newborn kitten at Strawberry Bank on Perth Road exhibited eight legs, but died very quickly. And of five kittens littered on 17 April 1860, one had two faces, two mouths, two tongues and two noses, but three eyes, the central eye lying on the junction between the two faces, so it was incomplete. The duo were quickly drowned.

It wasn't just feline freaks that the *Advertiser* was keen on. On 6 April 1838 a cow gave birth to a calf with two heads and two hearts (the farmer quickly buried it), while on 24 October 1851 there was a report of an extraordinary calf born one month prematurely on a farm near Dundee. The unfortunate animal had its vital statistics enumerated: two heads, two hearts, two pairs of lungs, two windpipes, two gall bladders, two livers, two stomachs, two vertebrae – and four legs. The two parts were conjoined in the middle of the back. Even more grotesquely, one calf had been dead for some time, its head being in an advanced state of decomposition. On 15 November 1844 there was a report of a five-week-old Newfoundland puppy in Stobb's Well with five legs: 'the leg is attached to the right shoulder, and both seem to work in perfect unison.' Something much more malformed was described under the heading 'A Monster Birth' on 6 December 1844. A puppy born in the Hilltown had 'a head resembling a horse's, its two fore legs shaped like the legs of that animal, and one of its hind legs bearing a close resemblance to a man's arm. The remaining limb was naturally formed.' The creature was killed soon after birth.

Hypnotising hyenas

Walford Bodie, 'The Wizard of the North', was one of the most remarkable showmen of his time. His on-stage acts included passing vast amounts of electricity through his body, conducting convincing but fake séances, and generally coming over as a Mephistophelean character – a reputation enhanced by his movie-villain looks and his cape, top hat and sinister moustache. In the *Evening Telegraph* for 14 November 1951 Harry Marvello recalled his experiences at the Dundee Theatre before the First World War, and remembered how Bodie, on an engagement in the city, came across an old decrepit lion that was on show for a penny a time at a local shop. Bodie came to an arrangement with the pitiful beast's owner, and soon photographs were appearing all over Dundee of Bodie 'hypnotising' the fearsome King of the Jungle. In reality, the lion could barely stand and was shot full of dope, but the publicity worked and the theatre was full every night. It may have been this stunt that prompted 'two well-known local gentleman' to challenge Bodie to come and 'hypnotise the hyenas and perform with the wolves' at an address on Castle Street, as set out in a piece in the *Courier* for August 1904. As far as I can tell there were no such exotic beasts at this location, and so the episode is either a joke or another of Bodie's manifold publicity gimmicks.

The Devil Crab

This is one of the more amusing – and ghoulish – animal stories from Dundee. Before the Tay steam ferries started in 1821, the river was crossed by vessels propelled by sail and oars. These ferries came in two forms – pinnaces (light boats with sails) and larger 'stout boats'. The latter were more reliable in bad weather but the former sailed more frequently. The routes and prices were strictly regulated, with the only official embarking and disembarking stations being Dundee harbour and Broughty Ferry on the north shore, and Woodhaven, Newport, Balmerino and Ferry-Port-on-Craig on the Fife side. Ferry-Port-on-Craig, now known as Tayport, is supposed to be the oldest ferry in Scotland. According to tradition, when Macduff was fleeing from Macbeth, he needed to cross the Tay but had no coins to pay the ferryman. He managed to bargain his way across using a loaf of bread as payment, and thereafter the jetty was called the 'Ferry of the Loaf'.

One of the Masters of the pinnaces was John Spalding, a tall, powerful man whose sobriquets 'Ballad Jock' or 'Cossack Jock' were awarded for his persistent singing of ditties that attacked Napoleon Bonaparte, then the scourge of Europe. He was much admired for his skill with the sails and his knowledge of the sea. But Sunday, 28 May 1815 brought a storm so fierce that it overwhelmed John's powers. His pinnace sank about half a mile from Newport; of the twenty-four men on board, only seven survived. John himself was seen to hang on to wreckage for a heroic time, before slipping beneath the waves. After five days his body was washed up on the Fife shore and taken to his home in the 'Craig, where it was, as custom dictated, laid out

The River Tay from the south in 1824, showing the pinnaces and other small craft used for ferrying passengers. *(Perth & Kinross Libraries)*

under a sheet sprinkled with rosemary and rue, while friends and sea-neighbours crowded into the tiny house. One of the visitors was a sixteen-year-old youth named Tom Hood, on a trip to see relatives in Dundee. Hood later became a well-known writer, and the curious teenager recorded what happened in the corpse-room (later reprinted in *Hood's Own* in 1870).

The space was crowded to capacity, but still everyone managed to keep a distance from the corpse. It was also dark, one candle already extinguished and the second guttering, throwing eerie shadows on the mourners. Then, to the disbelief of the onlookers – a disbelief that swiftly changed to shock and panic – the corpse was seen to move. Immediately people tried to fight their way through the narrow door, but Hood and others remained, unable to move because of the crush to escape. In the dim light a slow but purposeful movement could be seen under the sheet - 'proceeding slowly upwards, as if the hand of the deceased, still beneath the sheet, was struggling up feebly towards the head.' Those unable to escape the room shrank up against the wall in fear. Then came a weird rattle – and a large pound crab fell to the floor.

As the crustacean – which must have been lurking in the corpse's clothes, or perhaps in a more fleshy cubbyhole – scuttled across the floor, there were exclamations that the creature must be the Devil. Everyone pushed and shoved to keep out of its way, and as it headed for the door the press to escape its demonic presence was intense. The crab-demon made it to the open air and, no doubt scenting the river, scuttled down the little jetty. People jumped into boats or into the water to get away from it. It made it half way to the water when 'a little, decrepit, poor old sea-roamer' named Creel Katie grabbed it by the claw. In vain did the crowd urge her to release the Satanic partan, and, to the infinite horror of her neighbours, she took the crab to her hovel and cooked it in the shell. 'Someone said that a black figure with horns

The jetty at Tayport, where the 'Devil Crab' caused such terror. (This is the later pier, extended for the steam ferries.) *(Perth & Kinross Libraries)*

and wings and hooves and forky tail – in fact, old Clooty himself – had been seen to fly out of the chimney,' wrote Hood. 'Others said that unwholesome and unearthly smells, as of pitch and brimstone, had reeked forth from the abominable thing, through door and window.' Katie, unmindful of these rumours and simply pleased to have nabbed a free dinner, said it was 'as sweet a crab as any eaten' and had even improved the health of her age-wracked husband. But for many years thereafter the inhabitants of Newport and Tayport spoke in frightened tones of the day the Devil was seen in the form of a crab.

Gull-ible

Dundee's seagulls, fattened on fast food and discarded carry-outs, are notorious for their size and aggressiveness. Several urban legends are told of the city, possibly the favourite being that a gull landed on a balcony of one the high-rises in the Hilltown, quizzically studied the family dog, as if sizing the barking animal up – and then swallowed the hapless pooch entire. The standard story is that the dog was a cocker spaniel, but I don't believe a word of it – not even a Dundee seagull could handle anything larger than a Yorkie terrier.

five

RITUALS, RELIGION AND SUPERSTITIONS

Stone circles and standing stones

Urban development, official neglect and vandalism have eliminated or damaged much of Dundee's prehistoric heritage, but a few ancient ritual sites survive from the Neolithic and the Bronze Age (very roughly 3,000-1,000 BC). As well as their own intrinsic interest as relics of religious and ritual practices from an era long lost, these enigmatic and mysterious prehistoric sites often attract folklore and supernatural beliefs.

The only stone circle in the city itself is at Balgarthno, in Myrekirk Park, Charleston, just south of the Kingsway and west of Myrekirk Road (the Ordnance Survey National Grid Reference is NO35333161). Slap bang in the playing fields are nine large boulders formed in a perfect circle, although only one stone is upright. In recent years the circle has been enclosed by a metal fence, which hopefully will reduce the persistent vandalism and graffiti. A little further north, near the west gate of Camperdown Country Park, a small standing stone can be seen just west of the first green on the golf course (National Grid Reference NO355329). The green is called Druid, after the long-discredited belief that stone circles and standing stones were erected by the ancient priesthood (in reality these megalithic monuments pre-dated the Druids by centuries or even millennia). In the eighteenth century an underground passage called a souterrain was discovered near here, but this has long been covered over (see page 63).

Just yards from the standing stone is a cup-and-ring marked stone embedded in the west wall of the derelict West Lodge of Camperdown House – it was probably taken from the destroyed souterrain. Eight large cupmarks are visible, one of which is surrounded by two rings and a second by a single ring (although sadly the cupmarks have been filled in by cement).

Balgarthno Stone Circle, off Myrekirk Road in Charleston. (*Geoff Holder*)

Left: The standing stone on the Camperdown Park golf course. *(Geoff Holder)*

Below: Carved prehistoric art embedded in the West Lodge of Camperdown Park. Note how the cupmarks have been filled with cement. *(Geoff Holder)*

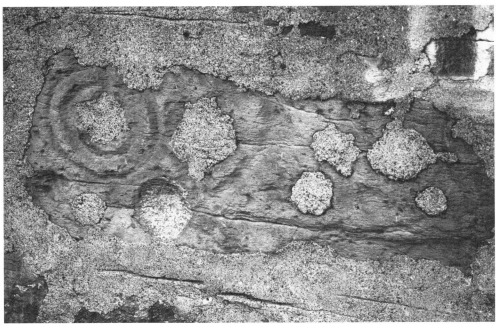

This is an example of prehistoric rock art. Quite what the cupmarks, rings, spirals and other symbols actually meant to the people who made them is unknown – suggestions have included agricultural counting, star maps, hunting directions, tribal markers, messages to the gods, representations of altered states under hallucinogenic substances, and much else. (As an analogy, the meaning of the 'Dreamtime' rock art of Australia is utterly obscure to outsiders; fortunately the Aborigines were not wiped out by the first European colonists, so there is still a living culture that can create and interpret the otherwise impenetrable symbolism. But with British prehistoric rock art, we are left with sheer guesswork.)

More rock art can be seen on one of the boulders in the Balluderon stone circle, which stands in a field north of the minor road between Tealing and Auchterhouse. There are multiple cupmarks, six of which have surrounding rings, some connected by grooves, making this a magnificent example. The circle itself consists of four stones, two of which are upright. Further west on the south side of the road by Old Balkello is a massive single standing stone about 9ft tall (NO36333830); part of the monolith had been split vertically. Several hundred yards southeast of the Old Balkello stone is the site of one of the more unusual monuments in the area. It was a rectangular enclosure surrounded by a ditch and a timber palisade, and has been interpreted as a mortuary enclosure dating to around 3000 BC. Here the bodies of the dead would be exposed on wooden platforms until the birds, animals and elements had removed the flesh (a process known as *excarnation*). The remaining bones would then be gathered for burial. Unfortunately the site, at NO37633723 near Wynton, is represented merely by a cropmark that is only visible from the air, all other above-ground remains having long vanished. Also in this general area is the carved Pictish stone known as Martin's Stone (see Chapter 4 for its dragon-related story), while further north-east, by the A928/929 junction, are the two Tealing stones, possibly the remnants of a stone circle (NO41643978). There used to be a stone circle near Greenfield farm in Auchterhouse, but the farmer dug it up to use for building dykes. As elsewhere, a superstitious aura hung over the ancient stones and the dykers refused to touch them, and the farmer himself met some kind of supernatural guardian which warned him to leave the stones alone – 'Gang ower the howe t'an other knowe,' it said, menacingly.

The Devil's stones

One day the Devil was minding his own business, standing on the hills of Fife, when he espied a small boat heading up the Tay. With his Satanic omniscience he knew the boat contained a Christian holy man by the name of Boniface, and that the saint intended to build a church where the Gowrie Burn met the Tay, and so convert the heathen Picts. Obviously the King of Hell could not suffer such a thing to happen, so he went in search of weapons with which to dispose of the pesky Christian. By the time the Devil had gathered together an arsenal of boulders, Boniface had started to construct the church, so four ballistic missiles were launched across the Tay. Sadly for the Devil's reputation, he was a lousy shot: two stones landed southwest of the church, another came to rest further east, near where Ninewells Hospital now stands, and the last sailed over the church to come to earth about a mile north. It is not recorded what the Devil did next, but I suspect something of a Satanic strop was thrown.

The only remaining Devil's Stone, also known as the Gray Stane or the Paddock Stone, can still be seen behind the conference centre of the Landmark Hotel, by the Invergowrie/

Above: The superb cup-and-ring carvings at Balluderon stone circle. *(Geoff Holder)*

Left: The massive standing stone near Old Balkello. *(Geoff Holder)*

The Paddock Stone, as thrown by the Devil at St Boniface. *(Geoff Holder)*

Kingsway roundabout – ask permission to view the stone at the hotel reception. Local architect and antiquarian Alexander Hutcheson collected the history and folklore of the stone in his book *Old Stories in Stones*. According to him, the boulder was originally part of a stone circle some 40ft across, made up of nine stones with a tenth within the circle. One of the fallen circle stones had a hollow in its upper surface called 'The De'il's Cradle'. After the circle was cleared away, the stone originally stood on the axis of three roads, but was later enclosed by a railing in the grounds of the house built by D. M. Watson of Bullionfield, who duly called the mansion Greystane (this mansion forms the basis of the hotel). The stone is also supposed to turn round on its end three times every morning when the cock crows at Balgarthno farm, although as the farm is now the Gourdie Croft restaurant and Premier Inn Hotel, it is perhaps understandable no one has witnessed this dawn pirouette in recent years.

The other stones chucked over by the Devil have fared less well. One was the 'Dark Stane' which was on top of Menzies Hill, off Ninewells Drive (NO36203105). It was a tall thin standing stone some 7ft high, topping a cairn or tumulus mound known as the 'Roundie'. A smaller piece lay nearby, said to have been broken off by a lightning strike. The cairn is still there but the stone was taken down in the 1880s, when the wooded grove surrounding it became, as Alexander Hutcheson put it, 'the favoured spot of gangs of roughs who congregated to play cards on Saturday afternoons and Sundays.' Both the trees and the stone were removed, the latter being broken up and used to mend the local roads. Ploughing turned up many bones all over the Roundie.

The final pair of Satanic stones were the Goors, Ewes or Yowes of Gowrie, a pair of natural stones on the shore of Invergowrie Bay. In 1800 the stones were below high-water mark, and so were regularly washed by the tide; but by 1826 the belief was that they were inching nearer to land every year. This was a bad thing, as a prophecy (sometimes attributed to Thomas the Rhymer) stated that: *When the Yowes o' Gowrie come to land, The Day o' Judgment's near at hand.* Obviously the end of the world, particularly if imminent, is of great interest to all and sundry, and in his book *The Popular Rhymes of Scotland* Robert Chambers noted that, 'it is a common practice among the weavers and bonnet-makers of Dundee, to walk out to Invergowrie on Sunday afternoons, simply to see what progress the yowes are making!' When the Dundee and Perth Railway was built along the shore, land was reclaimed, and the Yowes found themselves permanently on solid ground between the railway line and Station Road. Strangely enough, the world did not end.

As for Boniface's church, nothing remains of the original seventh-century foundation, but the location is still a Christian site. Sitting on the mound once occupied by the tiny Celtic church is the ruined sixteenth-century Dargie or St Peter's Church. It can be visited from Station Road, Invergowrie, NO35073015.

Souterrains

Another type of prehistoric monument in the area well worth visiting are the underground passages known as souterrains or earth-houses (the name 'souterrain' is French and means 'under the earth'). These subterranean structures date from the Iron Age (800 BC to approximately AD 200), and are conventionally regarded as being places for the storage of food. A number of

The ruined Dargie church at Invergowrie stands on the site of Boniface's Dark Age foundation. *(Geoff Holder)*

researchers in the 'earth mysteries' field, however, contend that the low, dark and cave-like passages were used for more esoteric purposes, such as initiation rituals or contact with the spirits of the earth or underworld. There is no evidence for this, but it remains a possibility.

Dozens of souterrains are known throughout Scotland, and three around Dundee are easily visitable. The Tealing souterrain is signposted west off the A929 (NO41223817). The curving passage, which is now open to the sky, is around 80ft long; excavation uncovered a fascinating miscellany – bronze rings, a bracelet, ten querns for grinding corn, charcoal, animal bones, a piece of second century AD Roman Samian ware, cinerary urn fragments, whorls, and remains of stone cups. As with Iron Age sites elsewhere, the number of querns suggests this was a ritual deposit, possibly an offering to a deity of agricultural fertility. The site's most spectacular feature is a large cup-and-ring-marked stone embedded in the turf south of the entrance. Both of these carved stones were from an earlier culture, the Bronze Age, and would have been hundreds of years old when they were re-used in the souterrain; perhaps there was a sense of honouring the ancestors. In the nineteenth century there was a report of an underground vault or passage by Tealing House in the village. This was supposed to have been beneath a small chapel attached to the house. The chapel seems to have been destroyed at the Reformation, and there is now no sign of the passage; it may have been a second souterrain.

Another cup-and-ring marked stone is in the wall of one of the huts next to Mains of Ardestie souterrain, reached by a path west from the B962 Monikie road north of Monifieth (NO50303444), while a minor road leads east from the B962 at Templehall to Carlungie souterrain, (NO51123597). Both are open to the sky and signposted. Excavation has shown that the souterrains were deliberately dismantled and filled in sometime around AD 200-250.

The Iron Age souterrain at Tealing, with the re-used piece of Bronze Age rock art. (*Ségolène Dupuy*)

This strengthens the view that the enigmatic structures were food-stores, as it is surmised the farmers were stockpiling their produce to sell to the Roman army occupying this part of Scotland as a frontier zone during the second century AD. When the Romans withdrew further south, there was no longer a market for surplus produce and so the stores were dismantled.

Holy ground and hidden treasure

The *Statistical Account of Scotland* for 1791-99 records a tradition that there was once an ancient chapel in Tayport, long before the village became a parish in 1606. Although there was no record of this chapel, the local belief was so strong that the supposed site was still regarded as holy ground, and, despite being in the middle of a cultivated field, was never ploughed. Also in Tayport, a chest of gold was supposedly buried under Tower Hill in times past, its legend recorded in an old rhyme:

> Here I sit, and here I see,
> St Andrews, Broughty, and Dundee,
> And as muckle below me as wad buy a' three
> In a kist [chest].

The Howff

This old burial ground was once the friary of the Grey Friars or Franciscans, founded in 1260. The monastery was destroyed in 1547 during one of the many battles that periodically engulfed Dundee, and after the Reformation the stones were taken to build a new abattoir and tolbooth, while the ground became the city's new graveyard, replacing the grotesquely overcrowded churchyard of St Clements (which is now under the City Square). The south wall was part of the defensive boundary that once surrounded the town. The street alongside the Howff used to be called Friars Vennel, which later became Burial Wynd, but that name fell out of favour for some reason and it is now Barrack Street.

The name 'Howff' is a curiosity, as the word is an old Scots term for a comfortable meeting place such as an inn or pub – hardly a description to be applied to a graveyard. Its origin comes from the time when the Nine Trades, the craft guilds of Dundee, used to meet in the courtyard of the Friary. When the monastery was demolished the Trades continued to gather to discuss business in the open-air cemetery, which could hardly have been convivial. So established was this practice, however, that the Nine Trades paid an annual rent to the Town Council for the privilege, and each guild had its own exclusive part of the graveyard – the Weavers, for example, met by the north wall. After almost two centuries this situation was finally rectified when the guilds built their own Trades Hall on High Street in 1775 (it was demolished a hundred years later). The small, slim pillar marking where one of the Trades met can still be seen in the western part of the graveyard – it can be recognised by the pile of coins on its upper surface, which are regularly added to for some unknown and possibly superstitious purpose.

As the noticeboard at the cemetery entrance discreetly puts it, 'Sepulture was discontinued in 1857.' By this point the Howff was so overcrowded with burials it had become a stinking and unhealthy open-air charnel house, and was replaced by the New Cemetery on Constitution Street. These days the Howff is a wonderful oasis of mature trees and mouldering architecture,

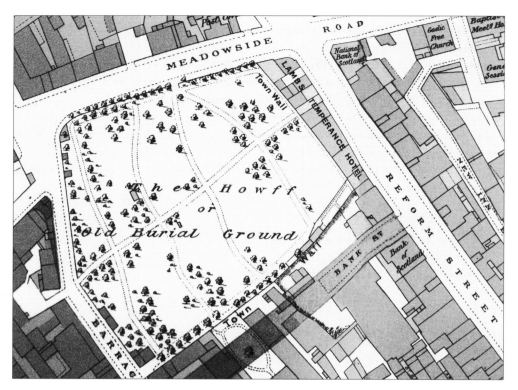

A nineteenth-century map of the Howff burial ground, showing the line of the old town wall. *(Perth & Kinross Libraries)*

The stone marking where the Trades used to meet in the Howff, complete with coins recently deposited on the top. *(Geoff Holder)*

bordered on two sides by the rear of tenements and offices, while the west wall still retains its fine blind arcading. The grounds are filled with the grotesque gravestone carvings that were the height of funerary fashion from the seventeenth to the early nineteenth centuries – it's the kind of place you can visit out of curiosity and emerge hours later, bedazzled by the sheer quantity of representations of trade symbols, skulls, crossed bones, skeletons, coffins, death bells, winged souls, angels, and King Death himself, often portrayed as the Grim Reaper with his scythe.

The stones are also famous for the many strange epitaphs found inscribed upon them. A few of these can still be made out, but others have eroded away and now only exist in the pages of Victorian books. Often they are meditations on death, such as the following on the tombstone of Thomas Simson, who died in 1579 (I have modernised the spelling):

Man, take heed to me,
How thou shall be, when thou art dead.
Dry as a tree, Worms shall eat ye;
Thy great body shall be like lead.

The time hath been, in my youth green,
That I was clean of body as you are;
But for my eyes now two holes been
Of me is seen but bones bare.

Another is an object lesson in bad punning, the deceased being Mr Alexander Speid:

Time flies with speed, with speed Speid's fled
To the dark regions of the dead;
With speed consumption's sorrow flew,
And stopt Speid's speed, for Speid it slew:
Miss Speid beheld with frantic woe,
Poor Speid with speed turn pale as snow,
And beat her breast & tore her hair,
For Speid, poor Speid was all her care.
Let's learn of Speid with speed to fly
From Sin, for we like Speid must die.

Or you can combine mortality with morality:

Remember man, as thou goes by,
As thou art now so once was I,
As I am now so thou must be,
Remember man that thou must die.
The memorial of the just shall be blessed
But the name of the wicked shall rot.

Typical eighteenth-century gravestones in the Howff. *(Geoff Holder)*

The Howff: the eighteenth-century gravestone of a gardener, displaying the tools of his trade. *(Geoff Holder)*

Reminders of death and decay among the tombstones in the Howff. *(Geoff Holder)*

Pithier epitaphs include:

> J.P.P.
> Provost of Dundee
> Hallelujah
> Hallelujee

Another from 1628:

> Here lie I
> Epyte Pie
> My Twenty Bairns
> My Good Man and I

And one Victorian collector claimed the following was found on a sixteenth-century gravestone somewhere in Dundee:

> Here lies old John Hildebrod,
> Have mercy upon him Good God;
> As he would do if he were God,
> And thou wert old John Hildebrod.

The fairy kidnapping

There is an old story from the Carlungie area that demonstrates that Scottish fairies were not the cute tiny-winged little darlings beloved of nursery tales. The Laird of Balmachie, an estate north of Carnoustie, visited Dundee for the day, leaving his wife ill in bed. That evening at dusk he was returning through the little knolls known as the Cur-hills, near Carlungie, when he came across a troop of fairies, pulling a litter with a human being on it. The laird knew fairies kidnapped people to be their slaves in the realm of Faery, and he also knew their dangerous reputation. Nevertheless, he rode up to the litter, placed his sword across it and exclaimed, 'In the name of God, release your captive.' The creatures immediately disappeared, leaving the shocked laird to discover that the litter contained his own wife, dressed in her bedclothes. He put her on his horse and headed for home.

Once at Balmachie he placed his wife under the care of a servant and headed to the room where he had left her that morning. There in the bed was an exact duplicate of the woman, to all appearances still suffering from fever, but complaining and fretful. The cunning laird built up the fire and, on the pretext of making up the bed, picked the supposed invalid up – and threw her on the fire. An anonymous Victorian collection called *Folklore and Legends, Scotland* described what happened next: 'She bounced like a sky-rocket, and went through the ceiling, and out at the roof of the house, leaving a hole among the slates.' Having disposed of the changeling, the laird questioned his real wife, who revealed that the horror had started just after sunset: A multitude of elves came in at the window, thronging like bees from a hive. They filled the room, and having lifted her from the bed carried her through the window, after which she recollected nothing further, till she saw her husband standing over her on the Cur-hills. If the laird had arrived just a few minutes later his wife would have been a permanent resident in Fairyland, and he would have been stuck with the bad-tempered fairy changeling.

Superstitions

'Superstition' is often a misused word, as it sometimes has a sneering quality about it – it is frequently applied to the customs, practices and beliefs of 'ignorant' people from the past, or people who we regard as less sophisticated than us, or people who are simply different. For example, when nineteenth-century Christian missionaries encountered the societies of the Pacific islands or Africa, they dismissed their complex religious practices, belief systems and symbolism as 'mere superstition'. The same dismissal was handed out to the Gaelic cultures of Ireland and the Scottish Highlands and Islands. The word, however, does have its uses, and it's shorter than writing 'customs, practices, folklore and beliefs' every time, so here are some 'superstitions' recorded around Dundee.

In 1892 an anonymous octogenerian published a small book entitled *Dundee and Dundonians Seventy Years Ago.* In it he recorded how 'Ghaists, death warnings and even fairies and witches were firmly believed in. Winding sheets and wedding dresses could be seen in the fire or in the old tallow candle with low wick.' When a death occurred in a working class house the clock was stopped – indicating that for the departed time was no more – and a plate of salt was placed on the corpse's chest until the coffin arrived for the funeral (salt was commonly believed to keep evil spirits at bay). If a hare crossed the road in front of someone they would turn back or take another road. If a cockerel crowed at the open door of the house, this was a warning that strangers would arrive later in the day. Hens that crowed, however, were 'not canny' and had their necks wrung.

Even earlier, the wealthy sixteenth-century merchants Robert Wedderburne and his nephew David noted down the 'evil days' on which no prudent man would commence a new task. In the *Compt Buik of David Wedderburne* we read his account of the effect of a total eclipse – the panicked people ran 'mourning and lamenting' into their houses so as not to see the terrible sight, and the crows and ravens took refuge in the steeple of St Mary's, inside the tolbooth and on ships' masts, a behaviour 'most terrible and fearful to all people young and auld'.

Cure by donkey

Superstitious practices are most commonly seen in the area of health, especially in times before easy (and cheap) access to effective professional medical treatment. On 24 August 1882 the *Aberdeen Evening Gazette* recorded a 'cure by donkey' from Lochee, where there had been a serious outbreak of whooping-cough:

A few days ago, two children, living with their parents in Camperdown Street, were infected with the malady. A hawker's cart with a donkey yoked to it happening to pass, the mothers thought this an excellent opportunity to have their little ones relieved of their hacking cough. The donkey was accordingly stopped, the children were brought forth, and the ceremony began. The mothers, stationed at either side of the donkey, passed and repassed the little creatures underneath the animal's belly, and with evident satisfaction appeared to think that a cure would in all probability be effected. Nor was this all, a piece of bread was next given to the donkey to eat, one of the women holding her apron beneath its mouth to catch the crumbs which might fall. These were given to the children to eat so as to make the cure more effectual.

Whaling superstitions

Whalers were another very superstitious group. The Master of the *Arctic* carried a huge George II penny that ensured a safe voyage with plentiful kills. Similarly, when the *Baleana* sailed to the Antarctic in 1892, the older women among the whaling families secured coins in the crevices of the rudder head. The fear of sailing on a Friday delayed the *Arctic*'s departure from Dundee for 24 hours. Protective horseshoes were nailed to the masts on the lower decks. If there was a problem on board the horseshoe was removed, heated in a fire and nailed up again. Sailors that died at sea were thought to be reborn as seabirds. Foxes were unlucky and it was forbidden to shoot one and bring the body on board. On one voyage the *Arctic* caught no whales so the crew burned the effigies of two of their number. Both men had been on ships that had returned 'clean' on previous voyages, and it was thought their bad luck was keeping the whales away.

The sailing ships were often becalmed, so various methods were employed to call up the wind. On one occasion the crew of the windless *Thomas* thought they had been bewitched, so one man burned part of his own clothing, saying, 'Burn the bitches.' Other fire ceremonies such as 'burning the witch' were common, and involved salt sprinkled onto a stick which was then thrust through the anchor and the salt ignited (this custom combined salt, iron and fire, all thought to combat witchcraft). When *Balcana* was becalmed in 1892 the crew tried calling up the wind by playing bagpipes; when this failed they threw a black cat overboard. Conversely, when there was too much wind anything that might make it worse was taboo: in 1885 a boy on board the *Perseverance* was smacked by a crewmember for whistling. 'Damn you,' said the sailor, 'don't we have enough wind now, without whistling for more?' The belief about 'whistling up the wind' was widespread among mariners of all stripes, but for the whalers it had a deeper and scarier meaning: on the rare days when the sea was calm along the west coast of Greenland, crewmen out in the small boats, low to the water, would hear a high-pitched whistling that died away to a much lower tone. The phenomenon was some effect caused by temperature gradients in still air, but to the whalers, surrounded by a hostile and awesome environment where God seemed very far away indeed, the eerie sound was a portent of supernatural doom.

The tidal harbour basin in 1909, with whaling ships to the right. (Perth & Kinross Libraries)

Water superstitions

On the morning of the first day of May, Dundee lassies would visit The Law and wash their faces in the dew, a practice supposed to ensure beauty and health for the next year (The Law itself is a natural volcanic plug that bears traces of an Iron Age fort, a possible Dark Age occupation, and a citadel erected by a besieging English force in 1547). People would seek their health by visiting the Nine Maidens Well at Pitempton (the one associated with a dragon legend – see chapter four), at the Lady Well in Auchterhouse and at the Ninewells on the old road between Dundee and Invergowrie; the name 'Ninewells' may be derived from 'Ninian wells', named after the Dark Age saint Ninian whose cult was revived in the twelfth century. These days, of course, the name applies to a splendid hospital.

A curious practice was recorded in John Ewart Simpkins' *Examples of Printed Folk-Lore Concerning Fife* in 1914. According to one correspondent, when the ferrymen on the Tay were beset by fog, they resorted to a compass made of straw: 'the seamen stuff the stern with straw… which they successively expose one at a time; and so supply it time after time from the stern of the vessel, till at length they arrive at the desired shore.' The actual process is not really described, so it may have involved using the straw to indicate wind direction; or it may have been something more esoteric altogether.

The case of the mysterious jars

Perhaps the strangest of all the customs associated with old Dundee is 'the case of the mysterious jars'. Alexander Hutcheson, whom we met earlier in the section on stone circles, brought these strange objects to wider attention in an article in the *Proceedings* of the Society of Antiquaries of Scotland in 1882. The previous year several old buildings on the south side of Nethergate had been demolished, and during the process one house, between two narrow passages called Scott's Close and Harris's Close, was found to have six jugs built into its outside walls. The jugs were all horizontal with their mouths facing outward, and had been clearly incorporated into the walls when the house was built. Further investigations found another old building on Butcher Row known as Wedderburn's Land, which before it was demolished to make way for Whitehall Crescent had the date 1684 placed on the front wall in huge figures. It was thought that the mansion was built by James Wedderburn, second son of Sir Alexander

Dundee from the Tay in 1793, with the conical hill of The Law clearly visible. (*Perth & Kinross Libraries*)

Wedderburn's Land (with the date 1684) before its demolition. *(Perth & Kinross Libraries)*

Wedderburn of Blackness. Here there were several jugs similarly placed at regular intervals beneath the sills of the upper floor windows, and many more in the inside walls of the external staircase. Hutcheson was baffled why someone had gone to the trouble of inserting numbers of otherwise ordinary jars into the fabric of these high status buildings, and suggested that it was 'some superstitious observance now forgotten', possibly connected with the belief that if certain birds nested in a building, it brought good luck to those living there.

Later writers such as Ralph Merrifield in *The Archaeology of Ritual and Magic* found examples in other buildings, including St Machar's Cathedral in Aberdeen, and wondered if the practice had started in churches as a half-remembered echo of the jars that had been strategically placed in large Roman buildings to help improve the acoustics. The suggestion was that some Roman structures were converted to churches when the empire became Christianised. This feature may then have been perpetuated when later churches were built as 'copies' of the originals. By the time of the Reformation in the sixteenth century, the original purpose of the jars – to improve the acoustics – had been long forgotten, and the practice of placing them in churches was dropped. However, people would have seen them in older churches, and by a process of association assumed the jars shared in the divine power inherent in the church. This power became degraded over the years to a simple notion of luck or protection, at which point domestic dwellings gained the jars as a protective device. To an extent this is speculation, as no documents exist to tell us what the architects and builders thought about the jars, but it remains a compelling possibility.

six

GOTHIC HORRORS: CANNIBALS, CORPSES, CRIMINALS AND CREATURES OF THE NIGHT

Cannibals!

Sometime between 1440 and 1460, an entire cannibal family was captured near Monikie and brought to Dundee for trial. It appeared they waylaid travellers, killed and ate them, the father boasting that the flesh of children and young men was the most 'tender and delicious'. The entire tribe was executed at the stake – with one exception, a one-year-old girl. She was fostered by a Dundee family, but as she grew older her inheritance came through, and she started biting her fellow children and licking their blood, eventually progressing onto actually eating morsels she tore off with her teeth. So when she had reached the age of twelve, she too was escorted to the market cross of Dundee for execution. A large crowd of angry Dundonians had gathered to jeer at her, but she turned to them and said, 'Why chide ye me as if I had committed a crime. Give me credit, if ye had the experience of eating human flesh you would think it so delicious that you would never forbear it again.' And thus self-justified, the cannibal child proceeded to the stake to be strangled and burned.

That, at least, is the story as told in *The Historie and Chronicles of Scotland, 1436–1565*, written by Robert Lindsay of Pitscottie in the 1560-70s and first published in 1728. Could it actually be true? The short answer is, we will never know, because it appears there is no more documentary evidence to support or contradict these extraordinary claims. However, sifting through the records might help us arrive at a balance of probabilities.

Much of the first part of Lindsay's three-volume work was a translation of an earlier Latin history by Hector Boece. Both Lindsay and Boece were criticised by later writers for their credulity, being accused of believing anything they were told and writing it down without fact-checking; by the late nineteenth-century most commentators were convinced Lindsay's cannibal story was entertaining fiction rather than factual history. Certainly some parts of his tale have a fictitious quality about them. He describes the dysfunctional anthropophagous family as living in a place called Dunfin, which he thinks was a corruption of 'Den-fiend', that is, the Fiend's Den, named for the cannibal *paterfamilias* himself. However, this derivation is nonsensical – A. J. Warden's historical opus *Angus or Forfarshire* shows that the location was already known as Dunfynd or Denfind several decades before the flesh-eating troupe turned up.

So, Dunfin was a real place, even if Lindsay's was not. Was the cannibalism real? Certainly eating human flesh is not a practice confined to pre-industrial peoples in the South Pacific, or to the survivors of shipwrecks or plane crashes. There are several documented examples of modern deviants in America, Europe and Japan who have killed and eaten people. In a Scottish context, there are three mentions in the historical record. The first was by St Jerome, who lived from about AD 347 to 420. This noted Biblical scholar visited Gaul (France) about AD 380, and left the following note: 'When I was a young man in Gaul, I may have seen the Attacotti, a British people who live upon human flesh; and when they find herds of pigs, droves of cattle, or flocks of sheep in the woods, they cut off the haunches of the men and the breasts of the women, and these they regard as great dainties.' In other words these 'Scots' (as the translation sometimes has it) preferred the shepherd to his flock. Note, however, that Jerome did not visit Britain himself, and so did not witness these atrocities; he may simply have been passing on anti-barbarian propaganda. Invading armies, from sixth-century Saxons to Germans in the First World War and Russians in the Second, have often been tarred with the cannibalism brush by fearful civilian populations; and when the Jacobites invaded England in 1745, mothers in Derby kept their children indoors, fearful that they would be eaten by the hungry Scots.

The second cannibal entry in the Scottish record is 'Christie Cleek', allegedly a butcher from neighbouring Perthshire named Andrew Christie, who, during a time of famine and desolation brought on by war, filled his stomach by dining on humans. Christie is mentioned in Andrew Wyntoun's *Orygynale Cronykil of Scotland*, written around 1420. The work is entirely written in rhyme, the relevant section reading:

A Carle they said was near thereby,
That would set settis [traps] commonly,
Children and women for to slay,
And swains that he might over-ta';
And ate them all that he get might:
Chrysten Cleek till name be bight.
That sorry life continued he,
While waste but folk was the countrie.

Wyntoun sets Christie's activities around the year 1339, when Scotland was suffering from the despoliation of the armies of Edward III. In many respects Christie Cleek pre-echoes the Dundee cannibals: according to later versions of the legend, he waylaid travellers (pulling them off their horses with his 'cleek' or crook), cut them up using his butchery skills, and cooked the flesh for his band of desperate followers who scavenged the Grampian foothills.

The third Scottish cannibal is the infamous Sawney Bean, who supposedly presided over three or four generations of murderers responsible for the slaughter and consumption of travellers in the fourteenth or fifteenth century ('the family that slays together stays together'). It is usually claimed that Mr Bean and his tribe were exterminated within their reeking cave by a troop of Government soldiers. This took place in Ayrshire. Or was it Galloway? Or Lothian?… Successive historians and researchers have failed to find any documentary evidence for the Beans, and nowadays the story is regarded as an early example of what are today called urban legends. I suggest there are so many similarities with the two earlier episodes that the Sawney Bean story is at least in part drawn from the writings about Christie Cleek and the Dundee cannibals. It is possible that the tale was first concocted in the 1700s as a piece of anti-Scottish propaganda.

Lindsay, however, was a patriot, and would not have wanted his readers to think that his fellow Scots were corpse-eating savages. So is the tale of the Dundee cannibal family credible? I suggest it is in part – there may well have been a nest of brigands out in the wilds near Monikie, and given what we know of human behaviour in desperate circumstances, they could occasionally have munched on roast *long pig*. As for the tale of the infant girl who grows up to be a cannibal just like her dear old dad – well that, it seems to me, is a fanciful addition tacked on because the original description is too bare, with not enough narrative to get your teeth into. I suggest therefore that it is an agent of *storytelling*, imported into the tale because *that's the way the story should end*. So although the story of the girl is almost certainly fictitious, the flesh-eating family is at least plausible.

I was a teenage cannibal bride

There is another tale of a Dundee lass in a cannibal family, and this one is fully documented. In October 1849 the Royal Navy survey ship HMS *Rattlesnake* anchored off Murralagh or Prince of Wales Island, a small speck of land north of the tip of Cape York, Australia, known to be inhabited by a fierce tribe known as the Kaurarega, whose warriors decapitated and ate their enemies. Among the crew was John McGillivray. To his amazement he was approached by a naked, scarred and heavily sunburned young woman with badly blistered skin. Recognising her strong Scottish accent, the astonished zoologist from Aberdeen asked, 'Are you from Dundee?'

Barbara Crawford was born in Dundee, one of the seven children of Charles and Jane Crawford. In 1837 the family emigrated to find a better life in Australia, settling in Sydney. But times were still hard and in 1843 three of the girls left to become domestic drudges. Two went to Western Australia, but eleven-year-old Barbara was taken by William Thompson, who lived near the harsh Brisbane Penal Colony at Moreton Bay in Queensland. The former convict scratched a living from salvaging ships; after a year, Barbara was promoted from servant to Mrs Thompson. In June 1844, when she was thirteen, Barbara joined her husband on a voyage to salvage whale oil from the wreck of a whaler, but their little cutter fell victim to the waters of the notorious Torres Strait. Thompson and the crew were presumably drowned, and Barbara was cast ashore on Murralagh Island. Under normal circumstances she would have been killed, but – in the kind of twist of fate that should by rights only exist in adventure fiction – she bore an uncanny resemblance to Gioma, the recently-deceased daughter of Chief Peaquee. The tribe recognised her as the reincarnation of the beloved Gioma, gave her the dead girl's name, and welcomed her into their life.

Over the next five years Barbara/Gioma became almost entirely tribalised, sharing the food, witnessing the roasting of the severed heads of the Kaurarega's enemies, and bearing two children to her husband, Boroto. Then Boroto was enticed away by another woman. Barbara beat her up in a fist-fight, but realised she was now exposed to revenge and hatred from her rival, and her husband was probably lost to her; with good timing, the *Rattlesnake* arrived shortly afterwards, and the eighteen-year-old requested she be taken back to Australia. Barbara's past – especially her 'shocking' partnership with a tribal man – was hushed up to allow her to live peacefully within the sniffy confines of white society. She was reunited with her family and died in Sydney in 1916, aged eighty-five.

These days Gioma is part of Kaurarega folklore, a ghost white girl who came from the sea and lived with the tribe under the chief's blessing. The tale of Barbara's extraordinary five years with the cannibals was disinterred by Australian writer Ray Warren, whose book *Wildflower: The Barbara Crawford Thompson Story* is a thrilling read, and deserves to be made into a film.

Invasion of the bodysnatchers

The growth of medical schools in Scotland from the late 1700s onward prompted a consequent increased demand for corpses to be used in the teaching of anatomy. Not enough cadavers could be obtained through legal means so medical students – or private individuals looking to make a quick buck by selling the valuable bodies – took to raiding graveyards and snatching away the recently buried. An example was reported in the *Advertiser* for 13 May 1824. Two men employed to watch a new grave overnight at Lochee cemetery were attacked by a pair of resurrectionists, but managed to drive their assailants off. A second assault on the grave was attempted the following night, but this too was frustrated.

There was no medical school in Dundee where the corpses could have been taken for dissection, so the suspicion was that the bodies were either being shipped to Edinburgh, or a local doctor was brushing up on his anatomy skills. To combat the 'Resurrectionist Men' a watching association was formed, with men tasked to patrol the Howff after dark. A watchtower was also built, to provide shelter for those cold winter nights. There were actually only a small number of attempts at graverobbing, so the watchers apparently helped pass the time by playing cards, telling jokes and stories, and taking the odd sip of whisky – purely to keep out the cold, you understand.

One of the few cases of an actual attempt to snatch a body took place around 1827, and was recorded in J. M. Beatts' *Reminiscences of a Dundonian* of 1882. A widower was in the habit of visiting his wife's grave at night, something he did every so often for some months after her death. At this point the graveyard was theoretically locked, but the wall was so dilapidated it was easy for anyone to gain entry. As the man walked past the unkempt graves, he saw the light of a lantern. His approach caused two shadowy figures to flee, abandoning the lantern, along with a pickaxe and shovel – and a sack containing a body. The widower reported the crime to the guard at the Town House, and a Town officer took possession of the body and tools. The next morning Beatts saw the body as it was being examined, and it was identified as a woman who had been buried a few days earlier. The family were informed and the corpse was re-interred. There was no direct evidence against anyone, but the crowd suspected 'a celebrated Dundee

The tower built for the anti-bodysnatching watchers in the east wall of the Howff. The tower is long gone, as is the hill behind it (now the site of Reform Street). *(Perth & Kinross Libraries)*

surgeon' who had a door leading from the north wall of his garden to the graveyard; there was also a belief that the doctor was in cahoots with Geordie Mill, a local gravedigger, and a satirical ballad was sung in the streets:

Geordie Mill and his round-mou'd spade
Is wishin' aye for mair folk dead,
For the sake o' the donnel and the bit shortbread
When he gangs wi' the spakes in the mornin'.

A porter cam' to Geordie's door,
A hairy trunk on's back he bore –
The Quentin Durward frae Leith shore
Brought round that very mornin'.

The trunk, 'tis said, contained a line,
Wi' sovereigns to th' mount o' nine –
The price o' a guid fat sonsy quean,
To be sent to Munro in the mornin'.

Now Geordie doun the toun did go,
To call on Robbie Begg & Co.;
These are the knaves wham they do show
What graves to houk in the mornin'.

The reference to a ship called the *Quentin Durward* from Leith makes it clear the belief was that the body was to be taken to Edinburgh, and 'Munro' was Alexander Monro, Professor of Anatomy at Edinburgh University. Monro came to major public prominence when he dissected the just-hanged corpse of bodysnatcher (actually, murderer) William Burke in 1829. The ballad may have been penned by Mill's neighbour William McNab, who had been employed as a watcher of the dead. Mill was suspended but not actually prosecuted for any crime. Robbie Begg, along with Tam and Jack, were Mill's accomplices in lifting the body. A 'donnel', by the way, is a container of whisky, and 'a guid fat sonsy quean' is a buxom woman.

Weird scenes at an execution

Professor Monro and J. M. Beatts also had bit-parts to play in the following case, a strange episode involving soap opera dramatics, murder, and a distinct whiff of the supernatural. On 21 December 1825 David Balfour stabbed his wife to death in her father's home in Murraygate, then calmly went to the burgh jail and asked to be taken into custody for murder, even waiting unguarded on the prison stairwell while the murder scene was visited and the warrant drawn up for his arrest. On his confession, he was duly sentenced to be hanged.

Apprenticed as a sailor at the age of ten, Balfour was press-ganged at fourteen and subsequently spent eleven years in the Royal Navy. Having made Margaret Clark pregnant he married her when they were both sixteen, and lived in the Seagate. When he was discharged from the Navy in 1813,

The High Street in 1834, looking west. When David Balfour was hanged this square was a seething mass of humanity. *(Perth & Kinross Libraries)*

he shipped on merchant vessels, leaving his monthly half-pay with Margaret when he went to sea. But she was repeatedly unfaithful, and embarked on a public affair with one of their lodgers, Alexander Hogg. As a result the couple separated and Balfour moved to Aberdeen for three years. A reconciliation was effected, and for two years domestic normality of a kind prevailed. However, at this point they were living in the port of Greenock on the west coast, and there Margaret fell for Torquil Macleod, a tavern-keeper. The bizarre upshot was that David and Margaret returned to Dundee, *without* their own young child but *with* Torquil's six-year-old son from a previous relationship. Not surprisingly matters did not improve, and after many arguments the 'cuckoo' was sent back to Greenock. Margaret cursed David for denying her the company of her lover's child, and kicked him out of the house. Balfour went and borrowed a knife from a butcher's shop, and stabbed her. He later said that if Margaret had not been in when he returned home, he would have used the knife on himself.

When the facts of the case came out Balfour attracted a great deal of public sympathy. The jury at his trial recommended mercy for what they saw as a crime of passion, and a petition was started to have his sentence commuted. Nevertheless a gibbet was erected outside the Guild Hall at the east end of the High Street, and on 2 June 1826 David Balfour calmly stepped out onto the scaffold and, with a white nightcap over his head, had the noose placed around his neck and allowed himself to be positioned above the trapdoor. One of the three ministers present spoke a prayer, and then there was the moment of silence before the executioner stepped forward.

The crowd held its breath. Despite widespread distaste for the event – which had seen many take the ferry over the river for the day to escape the execution-fever rife in the city – some 18,000 people, a third of them women, were crammed into the square, filling every available nook, cranny and alleyway. It was 2 p.m. on a hot July afternoon, and many spectators had been standing there for hours. The atmosphere in the overcrowded plaza was intense.

What happened next was described in the *Courier*, whose reporter had a bird's-eye view:

> The stillness which pervaded the assembled multitude was interrupted in a manner as striking and fearful as it was unaccountable. On a sudden, a movement was observed, towards the west end of the High Street, as if a bomb-shell or some object of terror had fallen amongst the crowd. The panic was communicated in an instant to the whole of the dense mass, which became agitated like the waves of a tempestuous sea. The scene which the High Street presented at this moment, viewed from the adjoining windows, beggars description. The rush to every opening which presented an outlet from the imaginary danger was tremendous. Large spaces of the previously invisible causeway were cleared for an instant, and as quickly covered again by another wave of the undulating mass of human beings. Men, women and children were seen overturned, sprawling and screaming in all directions. The hats, caps and bonnets, separated from their owners, were countless. Several made their escape through the railing in front of the scaffold, and others were forced through head foremost.

One of those jammed against the wooden palisade in front of the scaffold was the young J.M. Beatts. He thought he was in danger of being crushed, but because he was small and light he raised his feet from the ground and was carried by the press of the panicked crowd to the New Inn Entry, where he got his shoes back on the ground and made his escape.

At the time, and forever afterwards when the subject of what happened came up, no one could agree on what had been the cause of the panic. Beatts claimed that a crow flew over the scaffold, and the superstitious urge to escape the ill-omened bird was what prompted the chaos. Many people said they heard a noise 'like that of a carriage and runaway horses,' and had moved to avoid being crushed under the hooves or wheels. But there was no carriage, no horses, and only a few witnesses laid claim to having sighted the crow. And further, the *Courier's* correspondent and others saw the hysteria start at the west end of the square, the part furthest away from the gallows. The newspapers, meanwhile, stated unequivocally that pickpockets had generated the confusion, and dismissed the noise of the rogue carriage as simply the sound of running feet. 'But,' as Beatts wrote, 'many considered the occurrence as mysterious, and it was never cleared up to general satisfaction,' while A.H. Millar, in *Haunted Dundee*, stated that for many years people believed psychic forces had been at work, and spoke of one of the possible causes as being 'supernatural imposition'.

In retrospect, the episode can be seen as a clear case of 'mass psychogenic panic', where fear is speedily communicated through a crowd, even though there is nothing to actually be afraid of. Significantly, no one in the crowd had any idea what was going on, and they were hot, tired, squeezed together, and full of nervous anticipation for the moment the bolt was thrown and David Balfour headed for the 'long drop'. In these circumstances the slightest thing could have acted as a catalyst.

As it turned out, there were no serious injuries, and the crowd returned and settled down. Balfour had been tranquil throughout the episode, and at 2.50 p.m. he paid the price for his crime. After a time his body was removed from the gallows and sent to Dr Monro in Edinburgh, to be used as a dissectible corpse in anatomy classes.

Jock the Ripper

Balfour's execution was the first to have taken place in Dundee for twenty-five years, and was the last public hanging. The next criminal to suffer the long drop was murderer Arthur Woods, who in 1839 was dispatched on a gibbet built especially for him within the walls of the new Dundee jail. Wife-killer Thomas Leith suffered the same fate in 1847. And the last man to hang in Dundee, in 1889, was 29-year-old William Bury, thought by some to have been none other than Jack the Ripper.

The case is fully considered in Euan MacPherson's book *The Trial of Jack the Ripper*. Bury, a former horse-meat butcher, had strangled his wife Ellen at 113 Princes Street, and kept the body in the room for several days while he mutilated the abdomen and genitals, a *modus operandi* close to the five murders committed by the Ripper in London. The Whitechapel killings had commenced when Bury moved to London, and ceased when, for some unknown reason, he moved to Dundee. Was this coincidence or did it point to Bury being the Ripper? He had no previous knowledge of Scotland, or any acquaintances there, so it may have been a case of necessity, choosing any place as long as it was far away from London – Bury was running from debts and a reputation as a dangerous predator. In February 1888 in Whitechapel he slashed one woman's legs and genitals with a knife, and in the same year he stabbed an elderly neighbour and half-strangled another woman. He was also consistently violent to Ellen, and overall displayed an utter hatred of women. So we have a disturbed, malevolent misogynist who was skilled with knives, lived in Whitechapel during the time of the murders and mysteriously relocated to Dundee when things became too hot for him in London, at which point the Ripper killings ceased. In Dundee he then committed a Ripper-style atrocity on his wife. These links between Bury and the Ripper murders are circumstantial and intriguing, but not compelling.

But perhaps the most bizarre episode in the Bury case is the writing detectives found in chalk on a door at 113 Princes Street: *'Jack Ripper is at the back of this door'* and *'Jack Ripper is in this seller'* (the spelling and grammatical mistakes are as in the original). MacPherson examined the timeline of the murder and its discovery, along with who had access to the door, and concludes that the only person who could have written the words was Bury himself. (The other possibility, of course, was that it was scrawled by Ellen.) The oblique confession – if such it was – had no legal value, as it could not be proved who had written it; however, both the *Advertiser* and the *Courier* made great play of it, and were convinced Bury was 'Jack'. And later James Berry, the hangman who plunged William Bury into oblivion in 1889, allegedly told others he was convinced the man he had hanged was the Ripper.

MacPherson makes a thorough case for William Bury being Jack the Ripper, but ultimately it founders on any direct evidence linking the man with the Whitechapel murders. MacPherson considers Bury to have been a true psychopath, lacking any sense of empathy with others and displaying an immense rage against women. From his interviews with the police, and the recollections of those who knew him, he also seems to have been deeply narcissistic, and it is

DECLARATION

THAT THE

SENTENCE OF DEATH

PASSED ON

WILLIAM HENRY BURY

By the Right Honourable LORD YOUNG, one of the LORDS COMMISSIONERS of JUSTICIARY, at DUNDEE, on the 28th day of March 1889,

Was carried into effect within the Walls of the Prison of Dundee, between the Hours of Eight and Nine o'clock a.m., on the 24th day of April 1889.

We, the undersigned, hereby declare that **SENTENCE OF DEATH** was this day executed on **WILLIAM HENRY BURY**, in the Prison of Dundee, in our presence. Dated this Twenty-fourth day of April, Eighteen hundred and eighty-nine years.

JNO. CRAIG, Magistrate.
WM. STEPHENSON, Magistrate.
WILLIAM GEDDES, Governor.
DAVID R. ROBERTSON, Chaplain.
C. TEMPLEMAN, M.B., Police Surgeon.
D. DEWAR, Chief Constable.
JNO. CROLL, Assistant Town Clerk.

CERTIFICATE

OF THE SURGEON OF THE PRISON OF DUNDEE.

I, **JAMES WILLIAM MILLER**, Surgeon of the Prison of Dundee, hereby certify that I this Day examined the Body of **WILLIAM HENRY BURY**, on whom **SENTENCE OF DEATH** was this day executed in the Prison of Dundee, and that, on that examination, I found that the said **WILLIAM HENRY BURY** was dead.

Dated this twenty-fourth Day of April, Eighteen hundred and eighty-nine years.

J. W. MILLER, M.D.,

MED. OFFICER, H.M. PRISON, DUNDEE.

The poster advertising the execution of William Bury, claimed by some to be Jack the Ripper. (*Dundee City Archives*) possible he simply latched on to the Ripper's notoriety to add a glamour to his own squalid and vicious crimes. Verdict: Not Proven.

Jack the Ripper was still a name to conjure with in Edwardian Dundee. In March 1904 the newspapers reported the case of Robert Cunningham from West Port. Under the influence of liquor he attacked his wife and a female neighbour, threatening to 'rip her up'. At his sentencing – he was ordered to pay a fine of 30 shillings or suffer 30 days' imprisonment – he was described as 'a would-be Jack the Ripper.'

The skulls in the cellar

A mystery hoard of human skulls and other bones came to light when a tenement was being modernised in 1978. As reported in the *Courier* for 7 December, the workmen had found a number of packages in the cellar of the unoccupied building at 12 Rosebery Street – and when they started to pull them out, the casings split and the macabre cache spilled onto the floor. The police were called but after examination at the mortuary it was determined that the bones were 'of considerable age', and subsequent investigations showed they must have been in the basement for up to six years. Where the bones came from and why they were there remained a puzzle, but the working hypothesis was that they had been picked up from one of the several old burial grounds exposed during twentieth-century redevelopment, and had been kept as either a prank or for ghoulish interest.

The vampire that never was

In mid-October 1912 a sixty-five-year-old spinster named Jean Milne was brutally murdered at Elmgrove, her mansion at the corner of Strathern Road and Grove Road in Broughty Ferry. She had been struck repeatedly with a poker, and then left, bound and helpless, to expire of shock. The horror of the attack – and the mystery of the motive for the murder, because it was not a robbery – attracted massive publicity. One aspect of the case intrigued Charles Fort, the indefatigable cataloguer of all things strange and unexplained in the world's newspapers and periodicals. In his book *Wild Talents* he noted that two perforations had been found in Miss Milne's body, and speculated whether some kind of vampire was on the loose (Fort had been tracking crimes with vampire-like characteristics over many years, noting a small number of cases where the victims bore two puncture marks). This notion bit the dust, however, when the detective investigating the case found a two-pronged carving fork at the scene. By this point Miss Milne had been buried, and so the fork could not be matched with the wounds. However, holes in her clothing were consistent with the size and shape of the prongs, and it is likely the fork was driven into the elderly woman's body as part of the torture to which she was subjected. No one was ever arrested for the crime.

Frankenstein on the Tay

'It was the secrets of heaven and earth that I desired to learn.'

Victor von Frankenstein

It is a truth universally acknowledged that when something becomes successful and influential, many people and places will struggle out of the woodwork with a claim to be the inspiration for the original work. So it is with *Frankenstein, or, The Modern Prometheus*, first published in 1818.

The scientist-Baron and his creation have of course been with us ever since. Despite the well-known history of its creation – the teenage Mary Shelley dreamed it up during a famous literary ghost story-telling session on a stormy summer night at the Villa Diodati on Lake Geneva in 1816 – a claim has been made that the 'original' inspiration for the world's best-known science fiction novel came from, yes, Dundee.

Mary Shelley – then Mary Godwin – did indeed spend almost twenty months in Dundee, on two visits when she was twelve and thirteen years old, sent north to stay with friends of the family while the Godwin household sorted out its manifold personal and financial difficulties. She stayed with William Baxter, a man, like her father, interested in radical politics and non-conformist religion. Mary seemed to have greatly enjoyed her time in Scotland, and in the 1831 Preface to *Frankenstein*, she revealed how it was there that she did indeed start to develop her imaginative gifts:

My habitual residence was on the blank and dreary northern shores of the Tay, near Dundee. Blank and dreary on retrospection I call them; they were not so to me then. They were the eyrie of freedom, and the pleasant region where unheeded I could commune with the creatures of my fancy.

This was also when she started writing: 'I wrote then—but in a most common-place style. It was beneath the trees of the grounds belonging to our house, on the bleak sides of the woodless mountains near, that my true compositions, the airy flights of my imagination, were born and fostered.' And like many young writers, she was learning what kind of stories she wanted to create:

I did not make myself the heroine of my tales. Life appeared to me too common-place an affair as regarded myself. I could not figure to myself that romantic woes or wonderful events would ever be my lot; but I was not confined to my own identity, and I could people the hours with creations far more interesting to me at that age, than my own sensations.

So, although this may have been the start of Mary Shelley the writer, there is nothing here about the genesis of *Frankenstein*.

Miranda Seymour's biography *Mary Shelley*, however, suggests that the teenager was directly inspired by Dundee's whaling fleet and the witchcraft stories and folklore of the city. It's true one of the characters in the novel has a whaling background, and some of the most vivid action takes place among glaciers and icebergs. The notion, however, that *Frankenstein* was conceived in Dundee is I think a stretch too far. Nevertheless, despite the literary licence, Mary Shelley's early connections with Dundee are of great interest. Back in 1912, someone else obviously thought this as well, as a plaque describing Mary's visit to the Baxters was set up on the north end of South Baffin Street, on the site of The Cottage (which had been demolished in 1890). The claim made on the plaque that The Cottage was mentioned in *Frankenstein* is erroneous (it and Dundee were only referred to in the preface to the novel).

In a nice piece of historical coincidence, part of The Cottage's garden was later the site for the Royalty cinema in the 1930s. So it is possible that, on the very spot where Mary Shelley daydreamed her fantasies in the 1800s, twentieth-century cinema-goers thrilled to Boris Karloff portraying her monster in the classic 1931 film version of *Frankenstein*.

The plaque marking the site of The Cottage, where the young Mary Shelley stayed. *(Geoff Holder)*

South Baffin Street today; once Mary Shelley daydreamed her fantasies here, in the garden of The Cottage. *(Geoff Holder)*

When there's no more room in hell, the dead will walk the Nethergate

We finish the chapter with zombies – yes, the shambling, flesh-eating, brain-devouring undead horrors that mumble and munch their way through numerous horror films. In 2009 student Ailsa Lawson, inspired by the classic 'zombie horrors' of George A. Romero, *The Night of the Living Dead, Dawn of the Dead* and *Day of the Dead,* created a two-minute homage called *Dee of the Dead.* At the Duncan of Jordanstone College Degree show later that year Ailsa made up two actors as zombies and unleashed them around the Vision building at Seabraes, while members of the public scrambled to be turned into the undead. Ailsa described the appetite for being made up with injuries as 'face painting for big boys'. *Dee of the Dead* can be found online, and Ailsa is currently pursuing a career in make-up for films.

Dee of the Dead features all the key 'gore shots' associated with modern zombie films – shuffling and decaying resurrected corpses, evisceration, disemboweling and cannibalism. To make the grue convincing, Ailsa visited an abattoir in St Andrews to obtain animal lungs and oesophogea, and a litre of ox blood ('don't drink it all at once,' the abattoir worker joked). The zombies were made up with fake wounds and decaying body parts, while the shot of the victim being pulled apart was created by making a gelatine mould of his chest, creating a pair of fake legs, and making a false floor to hide his real body. At the key moment the ox blood was pumped out through a hidden tube, with Ailsa standing out of shot pouring the red ichor into a funnel. The 'flesh' eaten by the zombies was chicken in tomato sauce; a number of repeat takes were required, leading to some of the actors feeling decidedly queasy about future chicken dinners.

Ailsa Lawson and her cast of flesh-eating, brain-munching 'zombies'. *(Photo: Lyndsey Gray, courtesy of Ailsa Lawson)*

seven

MYSTERIES, ODDITIES AND WEIRD WEATHER

The 400 million-year-old nail

Sometimes the world of the paranormal and peculiar throws up individual self-contained mysteries whose weirdness continues to intrigue us. One such case is the mystery of the Kingoodie Artifact or the Kingoodie Nail. The basic story is that in 1844 the prominent scientist Sir David Brewster was informed that a rusted nail had been found embedded in a block recently quarried from the Kingoodie or Mylnefield Quarry west of Dundee. According to the report, the part of the rock containing the nail was hewn directly from the quarry face – in other words, the nail must have been there at the same period the rock was formed. At the time the rock strata were identified as being from the Cretaceous period (145-65 million years ago) but a survey in 1985 pushed the date of the sandstone bed where the nail was allegedly found back to the Devonian period (between 360 and 408 million years ago).

The oldest known iron artefact dates from around 5000 BC, and in an archaeological context iron has often decayed to the point where the only evidence that remains is a rust-coloured stain. Human beings of the species *Homo sapiens* have been on the planet for perhaps 400,000 years or less. How could an iron nail become embedded in a piece of 400-million-year-old rock? Answering that is a frustrating process, as no illustrations were made of the object, and the nail itself has not survived. All we are left with are the descriptions in the 1845 *Report* of the British Association for the Advancement of Science, of which the key part reads:

> The stone in Kingoodie quarry consists of alternate layers of hard stone and a soft clayey substance called 'till'; the courses of stone varying from six inches to upwards of six feet in thickness. The particular block in which the nail was found was nine inches thick, and in proceeding to clear the rough block for dressing, the point of the nail was found projecting about half an inch (quite eaten with rust) into the 'till', the rest of the nail laying along the surface of the stone to within an inch of the head, which went right down into the body of the stone. The nail was not discovered while the stone remained in the quarry, but when the rough block (measuring two feet in length, one in breadth, and nine inches in thickness) was being cleared of the superficial 'till'.

So it appears the nail was twisted in a 'Z' shape, with the point and head at 90 degrees to the main body. Only one inch or so of the metal was actually embedded in the rock, the rest lying against the rock surface below the overlying boulder clay. Most importantly, the nail was not discovered when first quarried, but only when the block had been moved to the area where the stones were dressed and worked, some distance away at Inchyra. Subsequent investigation showed that the block was handled and turned over at least four or five times between the quarry and the dressing area.

The gentlemen of the British Association for the Advancement of Science did not seem to try very hard to investigate the case, as there is no follow-up documentation and, as noted, no attempt to record the nail visually. We are also not told the name of the first person to find the nail, nor how Sir David Brewster came to hear of it, nor indeed how long was the gap between the discovery and the moment that Brewster turned up. Perhaps the scientists had come to the conclusion, as the minimally-available facts suggest, that the nail had become accidentally adhered to the block during the handling operations, and possibly even banged in by a mason's hammer. The Kingoodie Nail remains a minor entry in the literature of Out-of-Place Objects, but its origin is probably very mundane.

The case of the vanishing cutlery
Another singular oddity was reported by a Dundee resident to the magazine *Fortean Times* in March 2003. Several months earlier the man discovered that the only three table knives he owned were missing. They could not have been moved by anyone else as he lived alone; he had not been burgled (and even if he had, three cheap knives were hardly a tempting prize); so, just possibly, he had accidentally thrown all three out with the food waste. He duly replaced the knives with a sixteen-piece cutlery set from Tesco; but just a few days later four forks went missing – three from the new set, and one from the original batch. He went through his rubbish bin, to no avail, and could offer no explanation. Of course, the sceptical reader will counter that men living on their own are notoriously careless and untidy, and sooner or later the missing cutlery would probably turn up under the bed or down the side of a settee; but as the correspondent noted, 'It's the mundane nature of the disappearances that make it so sinister.'

Mystery fall from the sky
A further staple of the paranormal or Fortean files can be found in reports of mysterious falls from the sky – anything from fishes and flowers to sand and snails. On 5 April 1980 the *Courier* stated that earlier that day black strands of 'long straggly material' drifted down from the sky over the west end of Dundee, the fall lasting for at least a couple of hours. The strands disintegrated into fine black ash when touched. The fire brigade reported themselves baffled, as there was no fire in the city. The police, however, established that controlled burning of reeds had taken place in the Carse of Gowrie earlier that day. 'We can only assume this ash, or whatever it was, came from this source,' said a police spokesman. It was not proved that the reed-burning was the cause, of course, so perhaps something else weird was happening in the atmosphere that day.

Dundee's dark days
Two examples of truly extreme weather can be found in Dundee's records, and, as is usually the case, thoughts turned to disasters of Biblical proportions, even to the end of the world. The first

event broke on the evening of 11 August 1884, and the *Advertiser's* report from the following day's edition has an appropriate apocalyptic quality:

> The Egyptian darkness which came brooding over the land and turned day into night, the pillars of impenetrable cloud which might have hid behind their blackness the dread artillery of the spheres, the crash of thunder and blaze of light in which the clouds and darkness were finally dispersed combined to impress with their awful grandeur the least observant and sensitive of mortals. We are assured from many quarters that a multitude of good people felt the end of the world to be at hand, and were only assured that the earth would last a little longer when the gas was put out [that is, the gas lamps were turned on].

But this, it seemed, was just the warm-up act. The main storm hit after 11 a.m. on the 12th. The *Advertiser* the following day described how an immense cloud came across the river, presenting 'an extended front of darkness solid and straight as a wall.' By noon the city was as black as midnight in December, but the scene was given a truly supernatural hue by the lightstorm of lightning: 'an almost continuous glimmer of what appeared to be waves of pale flame made contrast with the blinding bolts beyond,' wrote the newspaper's on-the-spot purveyor of purple prose. The great mass of cloud was rent apart, 'revealing what appeared to be the whole horizon on fire. Balls of the most brilliant light shot out from the darkness above and broke into innumerable bolts of flame.'

For an hour, perhaps two, the effect on the city was traumatic. Traffic ceased. The cattle market closed for business. Many mills and factories stopped work, partly because so many workers left their machines to cower in the passages, or even fainted away. People on the street also fainted with shock. The central telephone exchange suspended operations because there was so much electricity in the wires that many phones in offices were tingling. A young man in Broughty Ferry was rendered unconscious by a shock through his receiver. Horses pulling the trams were so frightened they dragged the cars off the rails. A fractured gaspipe was set on fire. There was extensive flooding. Many houses, shops and other buildings were struck by lightning, while at least a dozen people in the Dundee and Angus area were hit by bolts, although none were seriously injured – the only casualties appeared to be several cattle at Liff. One report spoke of several fireballs bursting on the ground at Menzieshill and Lochee, and in several instances the lightning acted as an explosive, blowing items or structures apart.

The second 'Dark Day' took place on another summer morning, on 29 August 1930, and again the end of the world was nigh. Overall, this Dark Day was not as destructive as its 1884 forebear, but it has remained in folk memory as a genuine fear of the sheer power of nature. Between 11.30 a.m. and 12 noon everything was as dark as the blackest night. Shop window lights could scarcely be seen. Men labouring outside had to stop work for lack of light. Again, there had been an exceptionally fierce thunderstorm the night before, with continuous sheet lightning – 'the most terrific storm of thunder and lightning within living memory ... the atmospheric upheaval which startled east Scotland between the hours of nine and one last night will be remembered for years as the severest thunderstorm experienced in the present century,' said the *Courier*. The shops in the Hilltown were flooded and cobblestones washed out of the street.

But what made the noonday dark so memorable was the eerie *quality* of the darkness. A reader wrote in to the *Courier* on 21 July 1999, recalling how 'it wasn't black darkness, it was yellowish-green, sinister darkness.' Another reader, Violet McDonald of Carnoustie, remembered her mother had told her what had happened at the jute mill where she was working. The mill floor flooded so the machinery was turned off and the workers told to go home. But when the large factory doors were opened so terrifying was the rain and darkness that no one would venture out. 'They all stood and gazed in awe,' wrote Mrs McDonald. 'Some "wag" tried to lighten the situation by blowing a makeshift trumpet and calling that the end of the world had come. My mother and her young friends laughed, but some older women were in tears, thinking the world had ended.'

BIBLIOGRAPHY

Anon *Folklore and Legends, Scotland* (W.W. Gibbings; London, 1889)

Anon *Dundee and Dundonians Seventy Years Ago: being personal reminiscences of an Old Dundonian.* (James P. Mathew & Co.; Dundee, 1892)

Adams, Norman *Scotland's Chronicles of Blood* (Robert Hale; London, 1996)

Archibald, Malcolm *Whalehunters: Dundee and the Arctic Whalers* (Mercat Press; Edinburgh, 2004)

Barbour, John Gordon *Unique Traditions Chiefly of The West and South of Scotland* (Hamilton, Adams & Co.; London, and Thomas D. Morison; Glasgow, 1886)

Beatts, J.M. *The Municipal History of Dundee* (Winter, Duncan & Co.; Dundee, 1878)

———————— *Reminiscences of a Dundonian* (George Petrie; Dundee, 1882)

Chambers, Robert *Popular Rhymes of Scotland* (W. & R. Chambers; Edinburgh and London, 1841)

British Association for the Advancement of Science *Report of the Annual Meeting*, Volume 14 (J. Murray; London, 1845)

Carrie, John *Ancient Things in Angus* (Thomas Buncle; Arbroath, 1881)

Crumley, Jim *The Winter Whale* (Birlinn; Edinburgh, 2008)

Dorward, David *Dundee: Names, People and Places* (Mercat Press; Edinburgh, 1998)

Eunson, Eric and Bill Early *Old Dundee* (Stenlake Publishing; Catrine, 2002)

Fort, Charles *New Lands* (John Brown Publishing; London, 1996)

———————— *Wild Talents* (John Brown Publishing; London, 1998)

Fleming, Maurice *The Sidlaws: Tales, Traditions and Ballads* (Mercat Press; Edinburgh, 2000)

Gaskell, Malcolm *Hellish Nell: Last of Britain's Witches* (Fourth Estate; London, 2001)

Grant, James *The Mysteries of All Nations* (W. Paterson; Edinburgh and Simpkin, Marshall, & Co.; London, 1880)

Hood, Thomas *Hood's Own. The works of Thomas Hood, comic and serious, in prose and verse* (E. Moxon, Son, & Co.; London, 1870)

Horan, Martin *Fanny Who? Famous Forgotten Dundonians* (Lochee Publications; New Alyth, 1986)

Hutcheson, Alexander *Old Stories in Stones and Other Papers* (William Kidd & Sons; Dundee, 1927)

———————— 'Notice of the Discovery of Earthenware Jars in the Walls of Dwelling-Houses in Dundee, with some Instances of the Use of Jars in Architecture' in *Proceedings of the Society of Antiquaries of Scotland*, Volume 17 (1882-83)

Kidd, William *Dundee Past and Present* (William Kidd & Sons; Dundee, 1909)

Lamb, A.C. *Dundee: Its Quaint and Historic Buildings* (George Petrie, Dundee 1895)

Lythe, S.G.E. *Life and Labour in Dundee from the Reformation to the Civil War* (Abertay Historical Society; Dundee, 1958)

McGregor, Alexander *The Law Killers: True Crime from Dundee* (Black & White Publishing; Edinburgh, 2005)

McKean, Charles & David Walker *Dundee An Illustrated Architectural Guide* (RIAS; Edinburgh, 1993)

McKean, Charles & Patricia Whatley *Lost Dundee* (Birlinn; Edinburgh, 2010)

Mackie, Charles *Historical description of the town of Dundee* (Joseph Swan; Glasgow, and Smith, Elder & Co.; London, 1836)

MacPherson, Euan *The Trial of Jack the Ripper: The Case of William Bury (1859-89)* (Mainstream Publishing; Edinburgh, 2005)

Malcolm, J. *The Parish of Monifieth in ancient and modern times* (William Green & Sons; Edinburgh & London, 1910)

Marshall, William *Historic Scenes in Forfarshire* (William Oliphant & Co.; Edinburgh, 1875)

Maxwell, Alexander *Old Dundee - Ecclesiastical, Burghal and Social, prior to the Reformation* (David Douglas; Edinburgh, and William Kidd; Dundee, 1891)

Merrifield, Ralph *The Archaeology of Ritual and Magic* (B.T. Batsford; London, 1987)

Millar, A.H. *Haunted Dundee* (Malcolm C. MacLeod; Dundee, 1923)

Motherwell, William *Minstrelsy Ancient and Modern* (Alex. Gardner; Paisley, 1873)

Philip, Revd Adam *The Parish of Longforgan A Sketch of its Church and People* (Oliphant Anderson & Ferrier; Edinburgh and London, 1895)

Pratchett, Terry *The Wee Free Men* (Doubleday; London, 2003)

RCAHMS *Dundee on Record Images of the Past* (RCAHMS; Edinburgh, 1992)

Seymour, Miranda *Mary Shelley* (John Murray; London, 2000)

Simpkins, John Ewart *County Folk-Lore Vol. VII Examples Of Printed Folk-Lore Concerning Fife* (Sidgwick & Jackson; London, 1914)

Sinclair, Sir John (ed.) *The Statistical Account of Scotland* (EP Publishing; Wakefield, 1983 – originally published 1791-1799)

Thomson, James (revised by James MacLaren) *The History of Dundee* (John Durham & Son; Dundee, 1874)

Warden, Alex J. *Angus or Forfarshire the Land and People Descriptive and Historical Dundee* (Charles Alexander & Co.; Dundee, 1880-84)

Warren, Raymond J. *Wildflower: The Barbara Crawford Thompson Story* (Raymond J. Warren; Brisbane, 2008)

Watson, Claire-Marie *The Curewife* (Polygon; Edinburgh, 2003)

Watson, Norman *Dundee: A Short History* (Black and White Publishing; Edinburgh, 2006)

Wood, J.G. *Man and Beast Here and Hereafter* (Harper & Brothers; New York, 1875)

INDEX

Other titles published by The History Press

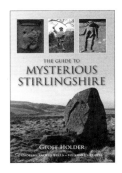

The Guide to Mysterious Stirlingshire
GEOFF HOLDER

This book offers an insight into the mysterious Scottish county of Stirlingshire, detailing the strange and uncanny in an accessible and enchanting way. Every historic site and ancient monument is explored, along with the many hidden treasures to be found in the area. Ruins, tombstones, sculptures and archaeological curiosities are complemented by 100 photographs, making this an indispensable companion for everyone about to journey into the mysterious realms of Stirlingshire.

978 0 7524 4768 1

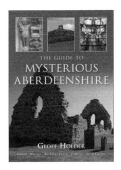

Haunted Aberdeen & District
GEOFF HOLDER

This spine-tingling volume includes Fyvie Castle, home to the Green Lady; Aberdeen Central Library, where the ghost of a former librarian still helps customers; the Four Mile Inn, whose staff have heard ghostly footsteps; and His Majesty's Theatre, said to be haunted by a ghost named Jake. Richly illustrated with over seventy-five photographs and ephemera, this book is sure to appeal to all those interested in finding out more about Aberdeen's haunted heritage.

978 0 7524 5533 4

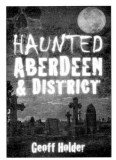

The Guide to Mysterious Aberdeenshire
GEOFF HOLDER

This guide offers an invaluable insight into the mysterious Scottish county of Aberdeenshire, detailing the strange and uncanny in an accessible and enchanting way. Every historic site and ancient monument is explored along with the many hidden treasures to be found in the area. From beautiful ruins, stone circles and eerie sculptures to the sinister-looking wickerman, this is an indispensable companion for everyone about to journey into the mysterious realms of Aberdeenshire.

978 0 7524 4988 3

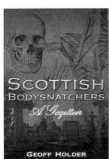

Scottish Bodysnatchers: A Gazetteer
GEOFF HOLDER

From burial grounds in the heart of Glasgow to quiet country graveyards in Aberdeenshire, this book takes you to every cemetery ever raided, and reveals where you can find extant pieces of anti-resurrectionist graveyard furniture, from mortsafes, coffin cages and underground vaults to watchtowers and morthouses. Filled with stories of 'reanimated' corpses, daring thefts, black-hearted murders and children sold to the slaughter by their own mothers, this macabre guide will delight residents and visitors alike.

978 0 7524 5603 4

Visit our website and discover thousands of other History Press books.

www.thehistorypress.co.uk